VATICAN II:
Last of the Councils

VATICAN II:
Last of the Councils

Foreword by

JOHN J. WRIGHT, D.D.
Bishop of Pittsburgh

HELICON Baltimore

Helicon Press, Inc.
1120 N. Calvert Street
Baltimore, Maryland 21202

Library of Congress Catalog Card Number: 64-23615

Imprimi Potest: John J. McGinty, S.J.
                    Praepositus Provincialis
                    New York, June 7, 1964

Nihil Obstat: Carroll E. Satterfield
                    Censor Librorum

Imprimatur: ✠ Lawrence J. Shehan, D.D.
                    Archbishop of Baltimore
                    July 31, 1964

PRINTED IN THE UNITED STATES OF AMERICA BY
GARAMOND/PRIDEMARK PRESS, BALTIMORE, MARYLAND

Foreword

The Ecumenical Council is a solemn gathering of many more than the two or three in the presence of whom Jesus promised to be found; it is, therefore, surely an event at which Christ is present. The Holy Spirit must dominate it. The Providence of God for his people must be constantly at work in and through it. The Council is the entire Church at work and the Holy Spirit is the soul of the Church.

All these considerations, and many more, make the Council primarily a theological event of supreme interest to theologians.

However, the Council brings together men, creatures composed of body and soul, even though made in the image and likeness of God. It takes place within history. Its divine dimensions transcend history, but its human components and participants make it the proper object of the historian's study.

For like reasons, the Council attracts the attention of the social scientist, one of the most recent and provocative newcomers to the world of scientific studies. It is inevitable that certain of the psychological and social implications of the Council would attract the interest of the trained sociologist and it is good that the first of these to publish his findings should be one who adds to his scholarly competence the training and insights of a priest.

Father Rock Caporale was present in Rome during the 1963 session of Vatican Council II not as a theological *peritus,* nor as a priest officially connected with the Council. He was present to study some of the human reactions and relations of typical participants in the historical gathering convoked by Pope John XXIII to make a twentieth-century contribution to the work of God entrusted to the Church. The human sides (sometimes the human limitations) of those Council Fathers whom he interviewed in the light of his declared purposes (all in accordance with the rules of the game in his particular area of intellectual concern) shine through the summary he has made of his findings. On occasion the reader is reminded of the obvious and yet often forgotten truth developed in one of Cardinal Newman's sermons: *Men, not angels, are the ministers of the Gospel.* Not less often, however, the discerning reader will be conscious, subtly but surely, of forces greater than human present around and within the work of the Council.

It is not Father Caporale's purpose or business to make either of these points. His concern is to study empirically definite phenomena which accompany the Council as any event which includes men, not angels, even though that event, as in the case of Vatican Council II, is concerned with the mysteries which God has given over to men for human exploration and exposition under the divine protections that surround the Council.

Theologians will reap the fruit of the Council for centuries to come. Historians will tell its story in the chapters of innumerable books until finally it becomes the material of eventual footnotes in indefinitely continuing books. Meanwhile, the sociologist has some interesting observations to make on the purely human side, if anything is purely human, above all in the Church. Father Caporale has made a good start along this line in the present intriguing, fascinating study.

✠ JOHN WRIGHT
Bishop of Pittsburgh

Preface

In the Fall of 1963, I had the opportunity to interview a sample group of leaders among the cardinals and bishops from all over the world who were in Rome for the Second Vatican Council. The interviews dealt with concepts and facts of specific importance to a student of sociology. Upon completion of the inquiry, it became apparent that the importance of the material collected for a doctoral dissertation transcended the limits of its original purpose and represented a close-up look at the leaders of the Roman Catholic Church today. In several discussions that followed on my work in Rome, many friends encouraged me to publish the results of my inquiry in the hope that this may prove a useful contribution to the effort at self-understanding in which the Church is now engaged.

With this goal in view, I acted on the suggestion and compiled this summary of the general impressions and ideas gathered in the course of my survey. For obvious reasons, I have avoided giving it a scientific garb: this may eventually be the task of another publication. What I intend to present here is the vibrant image of the Church, as I perceived it in the course of my contact with its leaders. I have tried to interpret this through a comparative analysis of opinions and facts. For each of the ninety respondents in my survey saw the Council in a different light, one which, at times, threatened to border on the hazy reaches of an idiosyncratic subjectivistic projection; although none in the least perceived his vision to be purely subjective, but rather felt that his view encompassed the Church in its best and purest form.

This book is intended to be of service to the Church, to the bishops, and to all who are interested in the success of the Council, for the glory of God. It aims to communicate to the bishops what their brothers in the episcopate think about vital conciliar issues. For many bishops it was not possible, for various reasons, to gauge the opinion of their fellow bishops while the Council was being held. In the course of my interviews with them, many wanted to know what I had heard or found out about other bishops' opinions, and many more expressed the desire to be given a copy of this summary when ready. In part, this book is an answer to such requests.

Some of the information contained here may appear somewhat delicate to put in print; even truth needs to be presented with prudence. For this reason, I have mentioned no names, and consequently the responsibility for all quotations given here must rest with me, though they represent in all instances the actual responses of the interviewees. In the course of these interviews, a bishop often would make a strong statement and then add: "This is what I think, but don't quote *me* as saying this."

Because I appreciated the necessity of such reservation, I agreed that no name would be mentioned in my published report. This, however, places on readers of my work a heavy burden of trust: trust in the honesty of my reporting and in the objectivity of my interpretation of the bishops' utterances.

Whether or not to concede this trust rests entirely with the reader. There are no vested interests behind this inquiry —only the urge to serve the Church with this seldom-used means of bearing witness to her, that is through scientific research.

I have conscientiously endeavored to render the thoughts and opinions of my respondents as faithfully as possible, as far as the circumstances of the interviews, the variety of languages in which they were conducted and rapid shorthand recording have permitted. Filtered through this in-escapable process of perception, writing, and translation, the final recording of responses can be expected to have an unavoidable margin of error. I am convinced, however, that this margin remains quite tolerable. Whenever gener-alizations have been attempted, they were made with cau-tion and appropriate qualifications. Throughout the work of investigation, I have tried to maintain the detached in-terest of the scholar, screening out the prejudices that in-evitably color one's images of personalities formed through exposure to reports purveyed by the mass media or hearsay.

The only identification occasionally given to my respond-ents is their nationality. This should in no manner be understood as an attempt to generalize about a whole group of bishops, since within each national hierarchy there existed extreme variations and divergencies of attitudes. This limited measure of identification is merely a device to allay monotony and a partial index of the variety of opinions encountered in an internationally representative sample.

The service intended to the Christian Community at large through this work may seem to some to be greater than the one rendered to the bishops; for these interviews make available to rank-and-file Catholics, in some cases perhaps for the first time, some of the thoughts and feelings of leading Catholic bishops from around the world. To this extent, the present report is equivalent to a confidential chat which a member of any diocese in the world might want to have with his bishop, in order to know more from him about the Council and its significance, in an atmosphere of informality, bridging as it were, for a few hours the dis-tance between bishop and faithful so commonly created by the differential status of the two.

Another group possibly benefiting from this report might

even be those in charge of the organization of the Council. Most of the content of this book may represent little that is novel to them, yet its publication here may serve as a factual confirmation of impressions and information gained on their own, and it may inspire thoughts of some practical value looking toward improved performance at a later session.

I would like to express a profound sense of gratitude to the ninety respondents of this study, the cardinals, archbishops, periti and observers, who cooperated so admirably with their time and their responses, and made this book possible. No words will adequately express the feelings of admiration and gratefulness I experienced in my encounters with them.

Sincere appreciation must be extended to Professors Robert K. Merton and Ivan A. Vallier, of the Department of Sociology, Columbia University, for their precious guidance and criticism in the course of this study. I must also acknowledge a special debt of gratitude to Donald R. Campion, S.J. and C. J. McNaspy, S.J. of *America* magazine, for critically examining the manuscript and for their valuable suggestions. For secretarial assistance I am indebted to the work of Miss Mary Ann Caporale and Miss Dianne McDonald, who partially transcribed the interviews on index cards and finally typed and edited the manuscript.

It is my sincere hope that this work will complement the mounting number of publications on the Council by focusing attention on the human background against which divine plans are actuated, and on the particular way in which the mystery of Pentecost continues in our times, where the Spirit transforms the human component into an instrument of truth and grace.

ROCK CAPORALE, S.J.

New York, Easter 1964

To the Catholic Episcopate of Vatican II,
Masterbuilder of a Church for the third millenium

"Then I saw a new heaven and a new earth. . . .
And he who sat on the throne said, Behold,
I make all things new. (These words I was bidden
write down, words most sure and true.)"

(Apocalypse 21: 1,5)

Contents

TABLES

VATICAN II:
Last of the Councils

I

Why This Study Was Made

The very presence in Rome of nearly 2300 bishops from all over the world was a challenge to any inquisitive mind: here was a supreme assembly of the leaders of one religious organization, gathered under conditions ideal for close-range observation, questioning and analysis because all were within easy geographical reach and almost all proved also to be psychologically and sociologically accessible. To approach a bishop in his own diocese, in an episcopal palace where he is surrounded by a host of subalterns and where, by divine institution and canon law he is spiritual ruler of the souls who live within the territory under his trust, is a feat that the observer feels often calls for a measure of courage and much good luck. In fact, few bishops would have the time to be interviewed in depth at home; fewer still would submit themselves to this detailed examination. It runs too much against the usual pattern with which they are familiar: that is, one of giving commands, questioning, passing judgment and correcting authoritatively. To this psychological obstacle must be added the physical impossibility under normal circumstances of conducting a survey of opinions among a body of bishops spread all over the world, men who are literally of almost every culture and language,

17

and who reside at such geographical distances from one another as to discourage even the most mobile research worker.

Although the bishops assembled in Rome were drawn from but one religious group, the Roman Catholic Church, they represented a body which is actually "catholic": that is, spread and active throughout the world. This character of genuine internationality and representativeness of the Council Fathers gives this survey a unique quality, for it is not customary to conduct a study with such world-wide representativeness.

Additional value accrues to the study by the fact that the people involved represent that highest stratum in a religious organization known as the *hierarchy:* that is, the leaders and commanders within a "sacred" society, with all the implications of spiritual power and its ramifications into the temporal and material domain as well. This, therefore, is a world-wide survey of the opinions and attitudes of the key religious leaders of the largest religious body in the world.

One could ask: why interview the *leaders,* the officials of the Roman Catholic Church at that, rather than select a sample of Church members in general, the rank-and-file Catholic the world over. This is primarily a survey of a changing Church, and today the primary instrument, subject and locus of change is the body of responsible leaders, not the rank-and-file Catholic. We confront here, in fact, one of the central outcomes of this study, a proposition of very general implication. The process of change in the Roman Catholic Church at the present moment acquires the characteristic of an inner renovation prompted and stimulated not so much by the lower strata, the popular layers of its membership, but by none other than the very top layers and the leadership group, in response to forces and stimuli from sources still to be identified and analyzed, (e.g., the impact of the intellectuals in the Church, or the effect of public opinion, etc.). This is a phenomenon that neither parallels nor resembles to any significant extent the processes of change within other large-scale organizations, and by itself constitutes a fascinating topic for study.

The third aspect of the study focuses on the nature of the process under observation, namely, the *process of communication* in the Church, which sums up and explains the events of Vatican II. The contention is that the common denominator of the events since 1959 in the Catholic Church is the changed process of communication in its widest meaning, implying an intensified and widely extended pattern of "dialogues" at all levels, and between the most widely-divergent units. The term "dialogue" was among the most popular and commonly used words during the Council, with reference to conciliar or Church events. Transposed and analogously applied, it served to characterize every innovation whereby a new attitude, a breakthrough or a novel approach to an old problem appeared. Little attention was paid to the etymology of the term; strictly speaking, it allows for only two parties to be involved in the encounter. Often the so-called "dialogue" referred to a complex interaction of multiple variables, people and institutions. (Trialogue or polylogue would have been a more appropriate term.) In spite of these shortcomings, the term and its wide use served to highlight the essential fact of the Church-in-Council.

We could construct a whole "theology of dialogue" and its place in the vast economy of salvation. Symbolically, the concept of dialogue is connatural to the agent of revelation, the Word. God's dealing with men took the shape of a Word, spoken, heard, accepted and acted upon in the person of Christ. The guilt that followed original sin was emphasized and embodied precisely in mankind's incapacity to "dialogue" with his master and God. The greater the silence between the two, the more bitter the guilt feelings. The work of Revelation-Redemption through our Lord Jesus Christ put an end to the silence between God and men. The dialogue was resumed, God telling mankind about himself and his salvific love and requesting a loving response from mankind.

Thus was guilt removed and mankind made to feel secure, in the hopeful joy of a loving father once again on speaking terms with his children. (Analogously, the young child in the family, unable to enter into dialogue with grown-ups whose world is so different from his own, develops guilt-feelings and complexes which he displaces into insubordinate behavior, delinquency, psychopathological moods and even neuroses: it all works towards stunting the natural and relaxed growth of the child; but a well-adjusted child communicates effortlessly with his parents, and his feelings of security are strengthened through this communication.)

Correlated with and consequential to the dialogue and to the intensification of communication in the Church, there took place a gradual attempt at structural modifications of far-reaching consequences which in their nature are homogeneous to the process of communication itself. This refers to the strengthening of organized national and international episcopal conferences, as a new and legitimized organizational unit in the Church, superseding the diocesan structure; to the liturgical reform as implying a change in the communicative interaction of the total religious body at the symbolic and worship level; to the emergence of conscious awareness of the necessity for the Church to reconsider her mission of evangelization and the way she is carrying it out, suggesting a wider and hitherto undreamed-of use of the means of mass communication available to modern society.

The common denominator of these three areas of change and reform in the Church is a trend toward decentralization, a shift in the distribution of power and status in the Church with the periphery (e.g., the laity) getting the largest share of attention and a greater degree of freedom and initiative.

The immediate conditions for such structural changes were not present before the Council, except embryonically and potentially. They have come into actuality through the peculiar atmosphere that the coming together of the Church's leaders has generated. And this, to any student of social phenomena, is a fascinating finding: the power, that is, of a human group to generate forces and processes never before dreamed-of by the individual alone. In this, we see one of the sources of the strength and resourcefulness of the Church—and, one might add, a part of the secret of her perennial youth—her communitarian aspect that guarantees her survival as a society, where the Spirit dwells and directs men and groups to their ultimate ends.

Methodology

This study was aimed at the achievement of three interconnected tasks: 1) identification of the present-day leaders of the Church in her effort toward change; 2) identification of the lines of communication; and 3) identification of the process of communication.

To initiate this particular kind of search, recourse was made to a "chain reaction" or "snowball" type of sample selection. First, some informal conversations and questioning identified four or five bishops who were considered outstanding leaders and representative speakers from among their respective national groups. These were interviewed first, reserving the option of discarding their opinions as items in the sample should a subsequent cross-check reveal that they were not widely accepted by their peers as outstanding leaders. Subsequent interviews disclosed, however, that in every instance those interviewed on the basis of this original choice were truly representative in the best sense of the word and would have been selected in any event had one started off with a totally different group of bishops. Thus, the pattern of an expanding network of leaders' names began to build up in the files, some being mentioned very often, some less frequently and others only occasionally. Bishops who scored high for frequency of mention by other bishops were subsequently visited and interviews requested of them.

At this point, troubles began. If interviewing as such is an art requiring skill and dexterity, interviewing bishops and cardinals poses a compounded challenge. A bishop is little accustomed to "giving an account" of himself and his thinking to an inquisitive stranger. His habitual relationship to others places him on a pedestal of authority. During the course of a day's work, a bishop summons others to answer his questions, gives commands, reprimands, grants permissions, corrects the wayward, judges difficult cases and makes responsible decisions. Seldom does he have to act as the recipient of questions that put a burden of answering on him, and seldom does he give to another person the faculty of passing judgment on what he says. A bishop is essentially a man of authority. The questioning confrontation of a sociologist with a bishop in some instances takes on the symbolic overtones relating to the age-old tussle between science and religion. This time, however, both factors appeared to be internalized to a great extent in the interviewer and in the interviewee. Science and religion appear to be questioning each other in person—a situation that is one of utmost interest and fascination.

In requesting each interview, the appeal was exclusively concentrated on two points: 1) that this was a scientific study, and 2) that the potential interviewee had been selected on the basis of the expressed estimation of other bishops on his outstanding representativeness in his group. In deference to the judgment of their peers, the vast majority of those approached granted the request. Only a few bishops refused to be interviewed, for one reason or another. An American prelate, for example, insisted that he did not intend to express his views on the Council, even for scientific purposes, before the Council was over. A South American bishop, after granting an appointment, thought it over and refused at the last moment. He seemed to have remembered making a resolution not to grant interviews, unless they were absolutely necessary. Four more bishops (a Frenchman, a Spaniard, an Italian, and a Latin American) asked to see a written copy of the questionnaire beforehand so that they could prepare their answers to it. Another asked to see the interviewer first in order to make sure that he was a genuine scholar (and a priest). He adduced as reason for this "security measure" the fact that there were many "false prophets" at large in Rome during the Council. . . .

The process of establishing contact and setting up these appointments offered an introductory view of the whole range of attitudes existing among the bishops with regard to scientific inquiry, interviewing, sociology, and the like. Some bishops, upon hearing that this was a study on the sociology of the Council, were genuinely pleased and enthusiastic. Others looked upon it as a quaint idea. Still others reacted with evident distrust and suspicion. On one occasion an Italian prelate, merely upon hearing that this was to be a study on the sociology of the Council, said with a somber face: "Sociology of the Council! You must be prudent because this can be very misleading." The warning was received with appreciation and turned into a request as to whether the prelate would consent to give his opinion and some advice on such a "dangerous" subject. He was already on the sample list, and this incident serves to exemplify how one appointment for an interview was made.

On the whole nothing but admiration and gratitude must be expressed to the 73 cardinals and bishops, as well as to the 17 observers and theologians who showed so much understanding of the efforts put into this study, and who generously agreed to cooperate by giving a precious hour, or more, of their time to answer our questions. Often the interview took place under the most unusual circumstances. For instance, it became necessary to accompany one bishop around Rome in his car, while he was paying visits to friends, in order to question him during these only free moments of his. On other occasions, repeated visits were paid to the place of an appointment, sometimes on the very outskirts of Rome, only to discover that the bishop had been called away unexpectedly for another appointment and had hastily rescheduled our meeting. But after traveling thousands of miles in and out of Rome, after hundreds of telephone calls, and hundreds of hours of repeated questions and answers, there was reason to be very happy: a bulging file contained written documentation of the views, opinions and attitudes of the Council's outstanding figures, a frank testimony to a Church which is renewing herself under the impulse of the Spirit.

II

Anticipating a Council:
The Threshold of Tolerance

The reaction of the bishops to the announcement of a council by Pope John XXIII was conditioned by their personal attitudes and expectations with regard to councils in general, and a council for our times in particular. The questions sought to elicit a bishop's conception of a council, its function generally in the Church, and more specifically its relevance to our times. Was there any need for a council? Did the bishops at any time feel the need for change in the Church, a sense that "something" must be done? And if so, did he think of a council as the mechanism for resolution of this need?

Without any hesitation and in deep sincerity, fifty-five of the respondents acknowledged that they had never thought about a council prior to Pope John's sudden inspiration. The reasons for not thinking of it or for rejecting its possibility reveal a whole range of set-ideas corresponding to each one's historical image of a council and its functions. A good many bishops acknowledged that they felt the need for some change, but hardly anyone linked this to the idea of a council. Some of their observations are as follows: "I felt the need for something but did not anticipate the possibility of a council so soon, because I thought of it as a very rare occurrence. I was greatly surprised." "I felt the need for some change, for I thought it impossible to solve the problems of the Church in the missionary world without a closer contact between the bishops and the Roman Curia. But I did not see how this could be done." "I did not know about the situation in other countries, but I felt the need for some *aggiornamento* in my country." "By temperament, and because of the formation I received at home and at school, I always felt the need for steady progress and for being open and understanding towards the viewpoints of others. I was spontaneously prepared for the council. But I had never thought of it in this way." "I did not think about the present ferment in the Church and the need to resolve it."

"I felt that an *aggiornamento* was called for, but that it had been initiated by Pius XII with the liturgical reforms, and thought that it would continue in this way." "Pope John's decision was a thunderbolt to us all." "I had thought that 1870 had put an end to the conciliar approach altogether." "While studying in Rome, I recollect hearing that Vatican Council I had to be resumed. Yet I had no expectation of a council actually being convened." "I had completely forgotten about the words concerning the council which are said at a bishop's consecration." "Pope John's decision was a surprise. Some of the cardinals did not like the idea. I wondered why the Pope chose the council to reform the Church. I admire his prudence in not intervening with his authority, but reserving the final decision to himself while permitting the bishops to speak freely." "I had been conditioned to thinking that councils were things of the past. I did not think about it at all. Then I thought, why not? Why shouldn't there be more councils after Vatican I?" "A council was a thing far off." "Nobody would have thought of a council back in 1958." "I never thought about a council, but when John announced its convocation we realized that it was necessary." "I never thought about it before and considered it to be impossible." "My first reaction was one of joy. I too had thought that Vatican I had ended the need for a Council. Even plenary national councils had gone into disuse. John had vindicated the council as a means of bringing the bishops' weight to a decision. This represents a departure from the old-fashioned authoritative intervention by the Pope with letters and *motu proprios.*" "I never thought about a council. I did not even feel the need for discussion. I think that this Council was too early. We are not yet mature. This Council should have come in the year 2000." "I never thought of a council. I thought I should let the Church go her own way." "Never thought of it. It may be too dangerous to have a council unless we afterwards put it into practice." "I did not even think about the need for some *aggiornamento.* We were so backward that we did not realize the need for it. When Pope John called a council, I was surprised and asked myself why and for what reason this was being done. After a month here in Rome, I said to myself that it is not such a bad thing after all. Now I say what a disaster it would have been had Pope John not convoked this Council." "I never expected one. Even after Pope John's announcement there were some people in Rome who wanted to postpone it. We too believed that Pope John could not make it by 1962 because we lacked the necessary preparation." "I did not see the need or the opportuneness of it, especially in view of the fact that with the proclamation of the primacy we had the means to solve our problems. I did not think it opportune because I did not see any doctrinal progress."

"Everybody thought that a council was a difficult, complex and impossible thing, especially because of Vatican I."

"I never thought a council was possible: we had no time to think about it. We would have preferred to have received orders directly from the Holy Father. It would have corresponded more to the Oriental family system, in which the Church is comparable to a big family which waits upon the father to tell her what to do." "I was thinking, in a vague form, about the resumption of Vatican I." "I did feel the need for some change, but never anticipated a council. It was impossible to voice your feelings: if you suggested changes you were looked upon as a Protestant." "I never thought about it. No one believed that it could be possible because there was still a ghetto mentality among the various groups of bishops. We felt self-sufficient, never thinking that our problems could be related to problems of other parts of the world."

"I have the impression that nobody among the bishops had any idea about it. John surprised us all, and no one knew what would happen in the Council. As a result of Vatican I, we were taught, and had imbibed the conviction, that councils no longer had a function in the Church. The idea of a council as a means towards desired changes did not enter our minds, although we knew that changes were desirable. At the back of our minds were the writings of the theologians." "No, I did not think about it. The common viewpoint was that a council was not possible because of organizational difficulties. When John announced it we were all taken aback with amazement. Now we feel that times have changed." "I never dreamed of it and never met anybody who had." "Although I wished for some changes in the Church, I never thought of a council because it is such a rare phenomenon and I always thought of it in connection with special events, such as heresy."

Since a majority of the bishops had clearly reacted in at most a neutral way to the announcement of a council, it

seemed important to note the few prelates who had thought
about or looked for a council. What had prompted their
interest or desire? What motivated their markedly different
attitudes? "Yes," said a bishop from Africa, "I thought of
a council, but not as a practical proposition, although a
good thing for the Church. The major difficulty I saw was
the great number of its members. From history, you know
how difficult it is to get all the bishops together." And an
Englishman said: "I did not think seriously about it. Occasionally we talked about the continuation of Vatican I and
the definition of the position of the bishops in the church.
But this was not seriously thought of until John came.
Many bishops were surprised. But their surprise turned into
joy and admiration once they realized that it could be
done." "We spoke about it in France. We thought it would
be particularly difficult, but necessary because of the crucial
problems left over from colonialism and among the poorer
churches."

Then came those who had a clear idea about the need
and the possibility of a council, and who also had a specific
motivation for it. "Ever since the definition of the Assumption I thought about a council, because the Church was
the only entity which could find the way to world peace.
I thought that our unity would have been a help to others.
I dreamed of a council; I desired it so much. I thought of
a council as a serious possibility. I thought it would be
useful as an encounter." More simply, a bishop from Latin
America stated: "I always thought that the only solution
to the problems of the Church would be a council, but did
not see its possibility because there was no man capable of
convoking it." "I thought of a council as necessary because
of the increase in communications," said a missionary
bishop. And a Central American: "I thought of a council
in view of the authoritarian approach and slow actions of

the Roman Congregations. The only way to bring about a genuine consideration of the needs of the Church was to gather all the bishops together. Since we need an internal renewal, the major process is to form new minds in the bishops." "I expected a council under Pius XII," said a German bishop, "because it had been too long since the last one. After his death, I did not think about it any more. The announcement of a council struck me like a bolt of lightning."

There was yet another group who had looked forward to a council, but to one that would be in the good old-fashioned tradition, that is as an occasion to anathematize a few more heretics and condemn some dangerous propositions. "I thought about a council when the *Humani Generis* came out," said an Italian bishop. "I thought the Church needed something to resolve the problems of rapid evolution and new intellectual ferment. There was much loose thinking and raw theology around. I thought that this should be exploited for its value, and at the same time that the faithful should be warned against errors." "I was thinking about a council, especially because Pius XI and Pius XII had been thinking about it, but not in clear and decisive form. Now I see that the council was not only opportune but necessary." "Yes, I thought of it while I was professor of dogmatic theology in a seminary and also as a bishop." And a Spanish bishop said: "I thought of it especially so that some clarification could be made about doctrinal principles and positions of the Church against neo-modernism, which is a serious danger to the Church today."

Thus, of the thirteen bishops who had, in advance of Pope John's announcement, given some serious thought to a possible council, nine had thought of it as a means of *aggiornamento* and solution of the problems which the Church faces today, while four had thought of it as the classic way of defeating errors by warning the faithful about false doctrines and anathematizing some heretics. Let us attempt to draw some conclusions from these flashbacks.

The first and most obvious consideration is the acceptance of a *council as a mechanism for the resolution of crisis and difficulties in the Church* implicit in the bishops' statements. But this conviction remained dormant until Pope John's personal and original decision brought it into reality. The hesitancy to be found even among those bishops who consciously thought of a council for a reform in the Church contrasts markedly with Pope John's courage and boldness, and points up the significance of this modern instance of charismatic leadership. It is clear that had the Pope disregarded his "inspiration," very probably there would still be no Council. All signs pointed to a passive acceptance of a long-standing situation, however unpleasant. An otherwise conservative Italian bishop commented: "We all were in crisis and were not aware of it. We had run aground. Only now we are seeing ourselves as we really are."

Most bishops, in fact, would agree that they had been desirous of some change. Such affirmations could, of course, represent the retrojection, to past times, of an attitude presently held. But the existence of some statements published prior to the convocation of the council, which expressed precisely these feelings, lends confirmation to such claims in some instances. We have already cited some of the reasons given by those who said they expected and wanted a council. For many, this was but a vague feeling, unexamined and unexpressed.

"I thought a council might be a good thing for the Church," or "I felt the need for some change" was the leitmotif of the majority of these bishops. "The idea of a council had been mooted for a long time as a desirable thing but never as imminent. Everybody saw the necessity of it, but not its feasibility." "The explosive changes in the world had been too rapid and the channels of communication in the Church were insufficient." "I thought of the need for some *aggiornamento* in the liturgy, and in seminary training." A missionary bishop stated: "I had thought of the need to accommodate the Church to the modern mentality, because of our changing situation from a missionary mentality to an indigenous one. Many Western concepts needed to be rethought and presented in Oriental garb. Many of the incongruities of the liturgy had to be corrected." "We had often spoken about and considered the need for change in the Church." "There has been too much distance between the missionary Church and the established Church. Now we are overcoming this in the realization that the whole Church is a missionary enterprise." "I thought that we needed some changes, especially with regard to coordinating the forces of the Church around the Holy Father, to keep them up to date." " I desired a renewal of the Church, a transformation; I wanted especially a new pastoral doctrine and attitude." "I thought about the ferment in the church and the need to resolve it." "I felt the need for some *aggiornamento*. The modern tendency everywhere is to dialogue. Modern man has become adult in his thinking. This has happened in the political sphere as well as in the spiritual sphere of the Church. The growing consciousness of the priesthood of the faithful is a sign of adulthood." And again, a Spanish bishop said, "I thought it was impossible to solve the problems of the Church in the missionary world without a closer collaboration between the bishops and the Roman Curia."

Against this vast consensus of opinion, six bishops expressed the frank and honest belief that there was really no problem and no need for a council in the Church. The reasons? "Because I saw no need for discussion. This Council came too early: it should have come in the year 2000." Or, "The Church should have been left to go her own way."

"We were so backward that we did not even feel the need of an *aggiornamento*." Yet another bishop thought that "the primacy definition was sufficient guarantee of *aggiornamento* in the Church." And a Chinese bishop said: "Let us face it. A council was not needed." Although these may sound now as minority voices, they must be taken as symptomatic of a brand of attitudes widely prevalent during the pre-conciliar period, and they testify to the changes brought about by the Council itself; for most of those who had not felt any specific need for a council prior to January 25, 1959, gladly admitted that in the light of present experience they had been in error.

The bishops' own words on this topic were quoted in order to stress that the *perception of a problematic situation does not coincide with a corresponding effort to find ways and means to resolve it.* For various reasons, faced with the need to examine and change, by far the majority of the bishops chose to wait and see, or even to accept the situation as it was, hoping for the best and leaving to God and to Christ's vicar on earth the task of doing something about it. Possibly this was the right solution under the circumstances. For one thing, the problems which individual bishops perceived may have far exceeded the limits of their power and experience. On the other hand, *because of the existing lack of communication,* no one was definitely sure how his neighbor bishop thought and felt on the same problem. Ultimately, facts and history proved that those who inclined to leave things to Providence were right in a sense: God did intervene. In the midst of universal astonishment and to the surprise of everybody, Pope John XXIII convoked the Second Vatican Council, thus taking the step that would bring about needed changes in due time and that would set a new course to history.

III

The Leader

Out of a general picture of hesitation, vagueness, and even confusion in the minds of many, the strikingly impressive figure of Pope John emerges as the man who, singlehanded, conceived and brought about the Council. His special vision and power, not given to anyone else, created, as it were, the final conditions that made the socio-psychological reaction "critical." Our questions concerning his part in the Council probed into three main areas: 1) how did the bishops view the personality of John, and in particular what did they think of some alleged contradictions in his personality; 2) what motivated John to call the Council; and 3) how did John feel about those who refused to go along with his innovating ideas?

The overwhelming majority of bishops, 64 out of 73, had nothing but praise and deep-felt admiration for Pope John. Only seven bishops expressed a critical or slightly unfavorable opinion of him, while two others expressed judgments that must be classified as at best indifferent toward him. The enthusiastic admirers of John's personality and action sang his praises aloud. They particularly admired his goodness, his charity, and his supernatural spirit, while at the same time many were ready to admit to an apparent contradiction in his personality. Here are some of the statements about him: "He was a man determined to do God's will at all costs," said a bishop who had known him for the last four years. "I have the most exalted idea of him. The apparent contradictions in him are explained by the fact that he was a man of extraordinary faith and accepted everybody in a simple Christian spirit. He tried not to do anything that would offend people, even those who disagreed with him." "He was a fatherly man, very attractive and realistic; not as intellectual as Pius XII, but he knew modern life deeply. Like a doctor, he saw what was wrong with mankind. His diagnosis was accurate. There were some apparent contradictions in him, for the very reason that he was searching for something. If one searches and seeks, one is bound to make some mistakes." A Brazilian bishop attested, "John was a charismatic man; he could be canonized today. He was a man of God and at the same time logical in his judgment of things. There was no apparent contradiction in him: it is we who are contradictory. John gave credit to secondary causes, however removed they may have been from his own mentality." A bishop from Australia: "John had a lot of experience, and because of his age he could talk openly and sincerely. He had seen life, and he had a grasp of people and things. He had only intuitions, though, of the needs of the world. Intellectually, he never thought through to the end of things and never formulated his thoughts. He was somewhat contradictory, formalistic, and traditional."

It is plainly evident that we are here confronted with a variety of attitudes and subjective interpretations of John's personality. None of the respondents, in fact, had had the opportunity to live close enough to the Pope to pass an objective judgment based on a long personal acquaintance with him. In a majority of cases, the judgment expressed was obviously in agreement with mass opinion based on the popular image of John XXIII. Each bishop traced his convictions to a relatively few personal contacts and, for the rest, to an appraisal of facts which frequently derived from press coverage and reflected the world-image of Pope John. This explains, too, the variety and even polarity of the judgments made about John. To some bishops he was a man of faith and love, with a simplified view of problems and people. To others, he was a very perspicacious observer who had made a deep study of history and men, and had found the right diagnosis of the ills of our time.

Although at variance among themselves, the opinions given by the bishops about Pope John have a limited range of variations and turn about a few leitmotifs. Nearly everybody agreed that simplicity, humility, and charity formed the central structure of his interior life, which overflowed and permeated even his human judgment and evaluation of people and events. A bishop from behind the Iron Curtain recalled how, when he crossed into Western Europe for the first time, he was presented with a basket full of gifts sent by the Pope. He felt this to be a very thoughtful gesture and he still keeps the basket as a remembrance of Pope John.

To other bishops it was his zeal and his patient understanding that deserved more admiration. "A man of heart, the parish priest of the world," said a Spanish bishop. A Latin American bishop was most impressed with his "respect for freedom and his sincere friendship. Pope John was God's gift to the Church to gain for her love and sympathy from the world, the prerequisites for the transition from apologetics to religious dialogue." The respect he demonstrated to one and all led him to "have faith in human collaboration more than we do. He was not capable of leaving out anyone who could be of service to the Church;

he built a spiritual democracy and accepted the collaboration even of those who opposed him." "Pope John was very
respectful of the opinions of others. In his charity he did
not wish to impose on anyone. This is the style of sanctity."
"John did not bother about minor things, but considered
only great ideas. His decisions were right. Actually, John
himself never thought of a council until the last moment."

It should be sufficiently evident that not all opinions
about John and his personality were simply favorable: some
were honestly critical and less than sympathetic. Two
French bishops who had been familiar with Pope John
while he was in France said that, although he had demonstrated a good grasp of things through his simple approach
and supernatural insight, he was taken to be somewhat
conservative and even a bit reactionary. He seemed not to
know what he wanted, but invariably would let his humility
and charity lead him. While in France, he profited considerably from this experience and opened his mind to new
ideas. When he was elected pope, some French bishops
nearly despaired and complained that the Church had fallen
very low from the heights of Pius XII. They accepted his
election only with the help of prayer and in a supernatural
spirit. Soon, however, upon hearing of his first unusual
gestures, they were pleasantly surprised and in a short while
totally changed in their view. This reaction to Pope John's
election was shared by bishops from other countries, too.
A missionary bishop acknowledged: "Upon hearing about
his election, I felt within myself: In whose hands have you
entrusted your Church, O Lord."

The French influence on Pope John was observed too
by an English bishop. "John," he said, "wanted to bring the
Church back to the primitive idea of a college of bishops.
He established a school for bishops. This idea came to him
while working in France. Unlike other hierarchies which

consider themselves as rubber-stamps of the Curia, the French and German hierarchies were more independently active. They have had many great churchmen, they consult the laity, they organize the bishops as a group. John thought of the Council as a school where the bishops could learn from one another's experience."

John's seemingly deceptive simplicity and apparent weakness were the subject of blunt criticism in some instances. Frequently, this originated from Italian bishops. "John," said one, "was a mystery and a phenomenon. Some of his attitudes left me perplexed. But he opened many doors, and this was needed. Perhaps he would have been unable to close them, however, should the need have arisen. He created a method without intending to do so. He was a holy man, no doubt." And another bishop: "It was an explosive pontificate. After that blast, however, we needed to settle down and appraise the results. John lacked both method and organization. His method was good for a time, but now a new development is called for."

Such criticism was by no means confined to the Italian bishops. A Canadian bishop concurred somewhat in this appraisal: "John was a deceptive figure: he did not think through the *aggiornamento* at all. He wanted the purification of the Church and the reunion of Christians, but he went no further. He was a strange mixture, an enigma. In certain ways, he proved to be a great traditionalist. Then he would suddenly turn around and make a revolutionary statement." And a Latin American: "Pope John was not strong enough to bring about a renewal in the Church. I don't understand why he did the things he did." A French and a Spanish bishop agreed that Pope John had a soft heart and that often, in order to grant the various and at times contradictory requests made to him, he would do things of which his intellect could not approve. "You could ask anything of him and he would grant it. He was generous beyond comparison." In addition, they suggested that some people abused John's goodness and patience.

A Latin American bishop concluded: "In the plan of divine providence, John was but an episode to break through the external impediments to the renewal of the Church. For a while, his intuition was good, but when the time for positive construction came, another person was needed, with the classical method, not just a charisma."

When the bishops were asked what motivations they attributed to John in calling the Council, the replies were more concordant and homogeneous. The question was what value they attributed to Pope John's claim of "divine inspiration" as the starting point of the Council's idea. Diplomatically, some bishops simply "quoted" him as saying that it was an inspiration; in so doing, they left the impression that they accepted this account. Others, perhaps ominously, declined to pass judgment on its objectivity. A few alleged circumstantial evidence and their own experience as proof that Pope John's idea had been a genuine supernatural inspiration. But there were also those who skeptically doubted the whole thing. One bishop denied it altogether on the grounds that he had heard from a cardinal that, long before the famous announcement in St. Paul's basilica, Pope John had spoken privately to him about a council. Whatever the reality behind it, its consequences were inescapably objective: he heeded his inspiration and called the Council.

But what specific objectives did John have in calling the Council? "John's major objective was a consultation with the Church." "He wanted all the bishops of the world to come together in order *to get the necessary information* on the world situation." Few bishops attributed this intention to him. The majority thought that Pope John's move was a well-planned strategy to involve the whole Church in his work for reform, and to overcome the Curia's opposition by using the world episcopate as leverage point. "He had an historical sense. To overcome the opposition, he attempted to make everybody interested, even those opposed to his ideas, to forestall a crystallization into an unsolvable situation." "He felt a certain inadequacy in the task of reforming the Church, because of his age." "He did not want a revolution but he wanted us to make one, later. So, he stayed out of the game and let things happen." "He did not like to command and to impose." "He was an optimist without bounds; he trusted that, if he called the bishops together, a consensus of opinion would necessarily emerge." Several bishops spoke of his intuition that in "collective situations the sense of charity has a greater force and prompts to greater profundity. He felt that this too was the characteristic of the modern age, and that it would grow in the Church."

A missionary bishop gave a similar, though stronger picture of John, strategist and at the same time holy man: "John came to Rome with a clean slate. He was wiser than we believed. He was aware of the power vested in him, but he was also a shrewd diplomat. Conscious that he could not do everything by himself, he planned to deliver the goods to a wider circle by means of a world assembly. A 300-year-old tradition had to be broken. He had to set himself free from the Roman Curia, a world apart from his mentality. This no single man could do. He was aware of the risk that many of the things he had done would in turn be undone by the Council, but he had the humility to accept this risk. He signed the *Veterum Sapientia* well knowing that it would be discarded. He made no mistake, for he was a clever angler. And in the meantime, he had to try and win over the dissident elements in the Church."

A very specific and somewhat surprising motivational factor, for several bishops, was the Pope's position vis-à-vis his own Curia. Said an Oriental bishop: "John convoked the Council because he could not get along with the Curia and was doing many things under pressure. We see in him a man of God and a prophet of the new era." "He may not have been very clever, but he had a sure sense of history," said an Indian bishop. "He was well read in many areas. He felt that the whole post-tridentine period had ended, and decided that the atmosphere of the Church had to change. But he felt powerless to alter the position of the Curia: he felt unequal to the task. So he appealed to the whole Catholic world. But although he knew that the Curia would oppose him at the Council, he needed the Curia's co-operation to organize the Council. I think he was *un furbone* [a very canny man]. He let bishops handle the situation, and events have borne out John's anticipation. To avoid a head-on collision, John chose the slow method so as not to compromise the Council."

An Irish bishop was of the same opinion with regard to John's historical erudition: "There was no simplification of problems in him. I have read the writings of John (I believe few people have done so) and found that he was no simpleton. He was deeply learned and had a great knowledge of the history of the Church. His study of the major figures in the Church from Trent gave him a long-range view of things and the confidence to make decisions. He looked at problems from a mighty height and saw them in terms of centuries."

Yet another factor commonly identified as one of the motivating forces behind Pope John's decision to call the Council was his evident reappraisal of his own role and of the role of the bishops. "Pope John," said a U.S. bishop, "vindicated the Council as a means of bringing the bishops' weight into the decision-making process in the Church. This implied giving secondary importance to old-style authoritative interventions through *motu proprios* and apostolic letters. John was feeling his way because he was using revolutionary techniques. His hopes for mankind could be realized only if all cooperated. He may have been too optimistic in his hopes, but he surely did the right thing." A missionary bishop concluded: "He wanted to get the greatest gain from the Catholic thought and experience."

An American bishop brightened his response with an unusual quip about John's motives: "It was," he said, "a supernaturally motivated caprice, or you may say, a studied caprice. John was humble, and only humble people can afford to be capricious." Noting that John had succeeded in involving in the Council even those who did not agree with him, he added: "John wanted an anvil to smash his hammer against. It was a strategy, a supernaturally motivated malice."

The bishops inclined to take a positive view of Pope John's motivation in calling the Council were agreed that "he knew very well what he wanted," that "he was a systematic thinker and had clear ideas." They also tended explicitly to exclude contradictions in his personality. "He was not a contradictory personality, and at his level of observation John saw no contradiction in what he was doing. He always kept a serenity of spirit and even an excessive calm, although he was not an administrator." "Pope John knew very well what he wanted. He was very shrewd and diplomatic. He had a great spirit of faith, but he was also a very practical man and knew how to get things done."

As might be expected, however, many other bishops disagreed on this point. "Pope John was not sure how the Council would work." "Maybe the Pope was confused about it: he expected that the Council could be concluded

speedily [*un concilio spiccio spiccio*]. But this was an illu-
sion. While he wanted a reform of the Church, he could
not find a simple resolution for the difficulties. Now we have
reached an impasse because Pope John did not have clear
ideas." A Canadian bishop, who was otherwise a strong
admirer of Pope John, recognized that "John was a deceptive figure. He did not think the *aggiornamento* through at
all. He wanted the purification of the Church and the reunion of all Christians, but went no farther. He was a
strange mixture, and an enigma. In certain ways, he was a
great traditionalist. Then suddenly he would turn and make
a revolutionary statement." An Indonesian bishop agreed:
"There were some contradictions in him. He was old-fashioned at times and very modern on other occasions." A
Chinese bishop calmly concluded: "John did not know,
himself, why he called a council. He said he was inspired,
but he may have been confused too. A council was not
needed; and he, like everybody else, was a novice about
councils, because the last one had been held almost one
hundred years ago!"

What was the real man like? Why, alone, among so
many who confessed that they had only played with the
idea of a council, did he take it seriously? Was it just luck
and adventuresomeness that made him the pope of the
century, or was it a deep sense of history on his part and a
profound knowledge of man? Was he really inspired, or
was the inspiration part of his master-plan to generate a
new atmosphere in the Church and in the world? The
answers to these questions may not be forthcoming for a
long time. To know them is actually immaterial: whatever
may be the real face of John XXIII, nobody could challenge
the fact that his personality has affected the history of the
Church as few men have ever before succeeded in doing.
It is the privilege of the great (and their sad fate as well)

to be so far above the average of mankind that, from whatever viewpoint they are seen, they should appear inconsistent and incomprehensible to less fortunate persons. In this sense, perhaps, there were no contradictions in John: it is indeed we who are contradictory, because of our mediocrity and superficial commitment to life. A pope who is proclaimed magnificently great by so many great bishops justly deserves the title of "greatest."

How Leaders Are Made: Charismatic vs. Bureaucratic

Pope John was elected to the chair of Peter on October 28, 1958. His announcement of a council came a few months later, in January of 1959. He was aware that the span of life remaining to him was very limited, and that he could not hope for a long pontificate. The striking character of his venturesome plunge into a council stands out the more by obvious comparison with the policies of his predecessor. Ever since 1950, the world situation had been tense but relatively stable amidst periodic outbursts of brush-fire warfare, indignant exchanges of diplomatic notes, and occasional troop movements. The Church situation had not changed considerably in the years that followed the Holy Year. And Pius XII had all the experience and information necessary. Why did he then shy away from calling a council? Did he ever think of it? Did he want it? These were questions we addressed to the bishops, many of whom began their pastorate under Pius and could be expected to know his sentiments.

The range of judgment as to a council under Pius XII extends from "utter impossibility," to "almost a fact, were it not for the constant danger of war." "Pius XII could have called a council, but had no time for it. Yet all the new policies of the Church are but an expansion of the policy initiated by Pius XII," said a Latin American bishop. "Pius XII had an authoritarian approach," explained another. "He would have been capable of convoking a council, but he did not think seriously about it." "I expected a council under Pius XII." "Perhaps Pius wanted a council but felt that the world was not psychologically prepared for it after World War II." "Pius had asked four or five theologians to prepare plans for a council, but it soon became evident that its realization would be difficult." "Pius XII is actually responsible for breaking the ice: but he was square and could not get through. John was round and got everywhere." "There was too much insecurity during the reign of Pius because of the recent war." "Pius wanted a council and the reform of the Curia, but this was only on paper on his desk."

More concretely, an Italian bishop thought that "a council was impossible under Pius XII. He thought about it but saw too many difficulties and implications, and did not have the courage to face them." Other Italian bishops confirmed part of his statement: "I heard that a study had been done about the possibility of a council. The conclusion was that the time was not mature for it." "Pius had asked the cardinals about it." Some bishops called our attention to the positive contribution made by Pius in the direction of a council. "I felt that the *aggiornamento* was initiated by Pius XII with his liturgical reform." "Pius was aware of the need for change and in his writings had tended in this direction, even with regard to the Curia." "Pius was slow to replace many officials at the Curia because he had in mind some kind of reform." "Pius thought of it but did not pursue the matter. However, he prepared the world for the Council with his analysis and with his new image of the role of the Church in every field of human endeavor; as also with the changes he introduced, however small, such as those about the eucharistic fast, and evening masses. They prepared the way for the Council. Pius' contribution should not be underestimated. He was ready even to reform the Curia."

As against these affirmations which give credit to Pius' good will and readiness, many others felt that the situation in the two pontificates was different. "It was not in line with his temperament to call a council." "Pius did not have any serious thought of convoking a council. I was in a high position at the Vatican then, and never had the impression that he wanted a council. He saw too many implications in it, and was frightened." "He was not the type." "I believe a council under Pius XII would have been impossible because of his temperament. He was not inviting enough." "Pius was not the man to call a council. He was too individualistic. This tendency he developed in response to the intransigent forces he had to face in the Church, particularly at the top." "I have a high esteem for Pius XII, but I also believe that a council under him would have been impossible. The encounter would have met with too much resistance." "Pius would not call a council. His was a one-man Church. Realizing that the Curia was inefficient, he ignored it almost entirely. He surrounded himself with some Germans as a substitute. He planned a reform of the Curia but was unable to fulfill it. I don't think that he believed in a democratic government." "I think Pius would never call a council like this. John was more democratic, while Pius was authoritative. Perhaps he saw better all the difficulties that would arise from convoking a council."

And so, objectively or subjectively, the image of Pius as desirous of and anxious about attempting a council, but failing to bring it into being, stands in the minds of many bishops. A further comparison will highlight the difference between Pius XII and John XXIII. The threat of war, political instability and ill health accompanied both popes during the last four years of their pontificates. So did the realization that their remaining life-spans were inevitably short. Pius in 1954, as well as John in 1958, knew that there were but a few years left for him to work and toil for the renovation of the Church. As for the social situation and the problems the Church faced, they were much the same in 1954 and 1958. Both men, moreover, belonged to the same era, John even being older by a few years than Pius. Pius could have looked to the Holy Year of 1950 as an indicator of the Church's readiness to venture along new paths; but he failed to exploit the surge of enthusiasm of that peak of his pontificate. Nor can we say that the Church was substantially more ready for a council in 1958 than she was in 1954. There remains, it would seem, but one conclusion, namely, that the difference on which depended the decision actually to call a council must be discovered chiefly in the characteristics and personalities of the two men. The personality of Pius was still under the influence of an era of authoritarianism, bureaucracy, nationalism, and post-tridentine mentality. John, on the contrary, had taken the step in his old age that projected him right into the midst of contemporary history. It made him think no longer of the past half century, but of the generation coming up in the year 2000. The approach was basically different and marks the pontiffs as identified with two different eras: Pius, the one that ended with World War II, and John, the epoch of the second millenium.

Several other bishops stated that Pius XI too had expressed a wish to call a council. Actually, in his first encyclical, *Ubi Arcano Dei*,[1] dated December 23, 1922, in recalling the 26th International Eucharistic Congress in

1. *L'Osservatore Romano*, December 26, 1922, p. 2.

Rome, he spoke about a council—but he spoke with hesitation, because he was waiting for a clearer sign from above, a manifestation of God's will. That sign never came.

The *Osservatore Romano* of November 4, 1959 (p. 3) reports a conference by Cardinal Ruffini at the Lateran University in Rome, on the first year of the pontificate of Pope John XXIII. In it the Cardinal revealed that, in view of the growing opposition to the Christian tradition, and of the confusion of ideas among the faithful, he had proposed back in 1940 that a council be called. Pius XII, said the Cardinal, took note of the proposal, spoke about it to other prelates, and did not dismiss it. Ten years later, in the summer of 1950, the Cardinal repeated his request, in an audience at Castelgandolfo, adding that a council would serve to counteract the many errors that were emerging in society. Even then, nothing was done. Father P. Leiber, S.J., private secretary to Pius XII, said that the Pope conceived of a council after the Holy Year. But, as the papal secretary added, he did not carry it out in view of his age, his temperament, and the international situation.[2]

In his address to the Council Fathers commemorating Pope John, his Eminence Cardinal Suenens chose as his theme: *"Fuit homo missus a Deo cui nomen erat Joannes"* ("There was a man sent from God whose name was John"). The Church needed a man sent by God, to turn history according to God's own plan and to lead the Church into a new era.

2. See Beat Ambard, S.J., "Das Konzil: das grosse Angliegen Papst Johann XXIII," *Neue Zuricher Nachrighten,* Zurich, February 7, 1960.

IV

The Episcopal Conferences: Action and Interaction

Because the bishops belonged to thirty-nine different countries, it was natural to give some attention to the organization of the episcopal conferences to which the bishops belonged. Up until the Council, where they existed they had been the only mechanism of collective action among the bishops. Moreover, during the Council, the conferences came into sharp focus and assumed a previously unsuspected role, especially in view of the new emphasis given to the concept of collegiality. The information here gathered embodies mostly a description of current facts and some proposals for future action. But at the same time, the comments point to one of the most important areas of eventual structural change in the Church.

It must be stated at the outset that conclusions arrived at in this study are valid only for the thirty-nine countries represented in our sample.* However, even the *Annuario*

---

* Here is a list of episcopal conferences covered in this study:

Asia: Philippines, Japan, India, Indonesia, South Viet-Nam, the Melchite Church.

Western Europe: Belgium, France, Germany, Great Britain, Ireland, Italy, Portugal, Spain.

Africa: South Africa, Cameroon, Congo, Madagascar, Rhodesia, Nyassa, Tanganyika.

Pontificio lists only a handful of conferences over and above the ones covered by this study, and most of those belong to smaller nations or islands. As a matter of fact, therefore, this study treats of almost all the major episcopal conferences in the world.

Historically, the dean of episcopal conferences appears to be the German conference of bishops, which originated in 1847: the national conference of the German bishops has been held without interruption at Fulda. However, the Irish bishops claim priority for their conference on the ground that it was "formally" organized back in 1854, at their first meeting in Dublin. They surely can claim the oldest statutes (1882) of any conference definitely approved by the Holy See. Around this time, the English conference began its meetings as well, but it never formulated its statutes until recently. They have been submitted for approval in draft form. From the bishops' statements, we gather that eighteen conferences were established in the interval between the first and the second World War (1917–1940), while fourteen more conferences were organized after World War II (1944 until today). What appears to be more interesting is that of the thirty-nine conferences studied here (and of the forty-five listed in the *Annuario Pontificio*), only seven sets of statutes were "definitely" approved by the Holy See—those of Austria, Canada, Colombia, Ireland, the Philippines, Spain, and the U.S.A. The other conferences either have no formal statutes at all and have built their conferences on an informal

---

Australia
North America: Canada, USA.
Latin America: Argentina, Bolivia, Brazil, Chile, Colombia, Ecuador, Mexico, Panama, Peru, Venezuela.
Iron Curtain Countries: China, Czechoslovakia, Yugoslavia, Poland, Hungary.

gentleman's agreement, or have statutes approved only *ad tempus* (that is, experimentally, for a limited number of years, after which new approval must be sought). It is perhaps mere chance that most of the countries having "experimentally approved" statutes are Central and South American countries, apart from Italy and Yugoslavia. This may be viewed as indicative of underlying difficulties in the growth of these conferences to maturity, but should not be considered a total loss in view of the fact that the temporary status allows necessary changes and revisions to be made, especially those that may follow as a consequence of the contacts and exchange of information among various conferences at the Council. From the above facts, one can readily see that the episcopal conferences as such are a relatively recent development in the Church and therefore it is no wonder that they have not yet crystallized into definite forms, but present various debatable aspects.[1]

Among the major points open to controversy in the structure of an episcopal conference is *the proper scope of its power*. Should a conference possess only moral authority based on a gentleman's agreement, and exercise mainly a consultative function; or should it be a juridicially established legislative body with binding force over individual bishops. As of now, no conference exercises juridical power binding on individual bishops: Rome has been extremely reluctant to recognize such power in any conference at all.

A second point open to controversy is the *composition of the conference*. Who should participate in it? In our survey, only twenty-seven conferences included all the bishops of the country: ordinaries, auxiliaries, coadjutors, and other titulars. The other twelve enforced some exclusion or other,

1. For the most recent and exhaustive study on episcopal conferences, see Fuertes Bildarraz' article in *Illustracion del Clero*, February-March 1964, No. 1000, Vol. LXII, Madrid.

usually of auxiliaries and coadjutors. Not infrequently also, some residential bishops do not participate in a conference's deliberations (as for instance in the classical cases of Italy, France, Spain, and India, where membership at the annual meetings is restricted to cardinals, metropolitans, and heads of regional conferences).

The third point of contention centers on the *form of accession to power positions in the conferences*. Major interest here focuses on the post of the chairman of the conference. Should it be filled by someone "ex officio," with the position going to the oldest archbishop or to the incumbent of a primatial see, or should he be elected? The question emerges again with regard to the members of the standing committee, or permanent board, or any similar limited group of executive members who have the daily task of administration of the conference.

Our inquiry reveals that only ten conferences elect their chairman and other officials, while twenty-one others have "ex officio" chairmen (customarily the primate or the dean of the hierarchy). We could not ascertain the precise procedure followed by the remaining eight conferences. The interesting aspect of these three major areas of dispute concerning the structure of episcopal conferences is that all three have come under heavy fire at the Council.

As for the right of membership, our survey reveals that bishops belonging to different conferences mentioned, among other desirable changes in their respective conferences, a wider and more universal participation by all the bishops of the country. This problem has now been decided by Pope Paul's decision of January 25, 1964, to the effect that episcopal conferences *must* include all residential bishops of dioceses, and *may* include coadjutors and auxiliary bishops. The question, however, of giving the conference juridical and legislative power does not find total support: from our sample six bishops would like more juridical and legislative power given to their conferences, while three other bishops would not like any such change. To this question too a partial answer was given by the Pope's declaration of January 25, 1964 that enactments of decrees by the episcopal conferences (with specific reference to liturgical changes) require a two-thirds vote by secret ballot.

The highest degree of consensus on proposed modifications of episcopal conference structure was with regard to the appointment of chairmen and officials. Ten bishops out of twenty-one, belonging to conferences where the chairman holds his post "ex officio," would like the chairman of their conference to be elected. They were openly critical of the ascriptive system of chairmanship, and found it to be a frequent cause of inefficiency in the conferences. Said one South American bishop: "In our conference, the initiative is always and exclusively with the president. Proposals and requests of minor bishops get no consideration. We would like a larger participation of bishops." Indirect confirmation that this was a not uncommon situation was given by the answers to our question as to whether the bishops of their group had contemplated any change in the conference, or whether they had reached any decision with regard to the application of the liturgical reforms to their country. Some bishops refused to state their position and answered that "this was up to the chairman to decide," or to the primate or senior cardinal who was the "ex officio" chairman of their conference.

In addition to the suggestions for changes expressed above, several bishops made it known that they expected other modifications to be introduced. Seven of them stated generically that various and momentous modifications were being contemplated or proposed in their conference. Two others said that they wanted more *decentralization,* while another bishop desired more *centralization,* because of the special condition in his country where there was a notable centrifugal tendency, and opposition to the center.

The general impression derived from the bishops' comments was that national episcopal conferences were still largely in an emergent and fluid stage. It is quite possible that the post-conciliar type of episcopal conference may scarcely resemble the pattern of those which existed up until the time of the Council.

Still missing and needed is a theoretical foundation legitimizing the status of a conference that would implicitly assign to a nation the rank of an organizational unit in the Church. More work will have to be done on a clear definition of the function of a conference, the scope of its authority, the degree of binding power of its decision, the extension of its membership and, equally important, the relationships of individual national conferences among themselves and with the center. Particular and marginal issues such as, on the one hand, the grouping of a number of conferences according to linguistic similarity, or consolidation of smaller conferences of various nations into area conferences and, on the other hand, splitting of larger and unwieldy conferences into several smaller ones, should be considered at an opportune time, before awkward difficulties manage to arise and grow. Is the national dimension the best and only basis according to which the conference should be organized? What is the optimum number of participants for an efficient conference? What is the relationship between a conference and diocesan synods? There is no doubt, many bishops feel, that this emerging form of episcopal organization will require much conscious study and planning, if it is to play a properly decisive role in the structure of the Church.

Because this study focused chiefly on the system of communication in the Church, analysis of the interaction process between bishops at the personal and official levels brought out two crucial factors. An attempt was made to identify and compare the frequency and intensity of contacts between groups of bishops (episcopal conferences), between individual bishops in a given conference and between individual bishops belonging to different conferences. The hypothesis was that the Council had laid down the conditions for an unprecedented intensification and even structural modification of the existing pattern of communication among bishops, and that this change constituted a source of various other changes that have begun to emerge in the Church. To test this, a double comparison of contacts between bishops, before and after, would seem the most readily indicated path to follow. We can consider the process first in numerical and, as far as possible quantitative, terms; then it will be possible to attempt a qualitative evaluation of it.

Before the Council, a large number of conferences (20 out of 39) met but once a year, while only six met twice a year or more frequently. Five more conferences met but once in two or more years (that is, up to five years), and one particular conference, the Italian, had never before met at all as a complete body of bishops. The change in the frequency with which meetings were held before the Council and during the first two conciliar sessions is strikingly revealed by the comparative table on page 56.

The difference in the intensity of communications is obviously of major proportions. What is more important, however, is that all bishops participated in the meetings during the Council, an arrangement that did not exist at the regular annual meetings of the conferences in several cases because they were open to only a selected number

Table I. Comparative Frequency of Meetings of Episcopal Conferences before and during the Council.

BEFORE THE COUNCIL		DURING THE COUNCIL	
Frequency of Meetings	*Number of Conferences*	*Frequency of Meetings*	*Number of Conferences*
Once a year......	21	Twice a week.....	5
Twice a year or more........	6	Once a week......	22
Once in two or more years.....	5	Once a week, or whenever necessary, or	
Never before......	1	now and then...	12
Not ascertained...	6		
Total......	39	Total......	39

of ranking bishops. Moreover, though there may have been some cases of absenteeism from conference meetings during the Council, this seems never to have amounted to more than a minor fraction of the total number of bishops in a given conference. Furthermore, the absenteeism phenomenon was not found among all episcopal groups, but only among those groups which were characterized by a stronger polarization of divergent ideological currents. The meetings dealt primarily with conciliar agenda, but part of their time was devoted to the analysis and solution of problems and difficulties back home.

There is no doubt that these meetings created strong group-feelings and also helped the various episcopates to see themselves in a clearer perspective by comparison with other episcopates. Of special interest was the development of group activity among two of the largest episcopates, the American and the Italian.

Prior to the Council, the Italian episcopate, nearly 400 strong, had never known what an episcopal conference was. Officially, there was the organization of the Italian bishops, the CEI (Conferenza Episcopale Italiana). It was started in 1951–52 and had its first meeting in Florence. Because of the large number of bishops in Italy, the only participants of the CEI were the heads of Regional Episcopal Conferences for the ecclesiastical regions of Italy, the Apostolic Nuncio to Italy, and two other members. In all there were twenty-three participants who represented the episcopal oligarchy of Italy. In the former edition of the conference's statutes, the chairman was "ex officio" the senior cardinal. To convoke all the bishops of Italy was considered next to impossible, and their large number was the perennial reason for never seriously considering such a meeting. The understructure of the conference was to be the regional conferences. These formed the first level and provided a wider base for consultation and information; the deliberative function was confided to the upper level composed of members of the CEI. However, with a few exceptions, as for instance, the Venetian Regional Conference, the regional conferences could hardly be said to have worked as expected. In spite of being provided with provisional statutes, in the opinion of our respondents, the CEI never functioned effectively and was practically non-existent. Yet it managed in the first decade of its life to change its statutes. In the new (still provisional) edition, the chairman is no longer the senior cardinal, but is appointed directly by the Holy Father.

The problem of the chairman is an essential and crucial one in the structure of the conference. Unlike all other conferences, the Italian bishops consider Rome as part of the area comprised by their conference. But the Bishop of Rome is the Pope and there can be no question of the Holy Father occupying his place in the conference. However, once the Pope is the central figure of the Italian episcopate, both as Bishop of Rome and, unquestionably, as Pope, there is little significance in the Italian bishops gathering to analyze their problems. It seemed evident to all that the Holy Father would take this position in the name of and for all the Italian bishops, using the large facilities available in Rome. Furthermore, the proximity of most Italian dioceses to Rome made recourse to the Vatican a far easier and quicker route to the solution of a given problem than a deliberative gathering of all the bishops.

Communication between the various dioceses and the center was easy and frequent in Italy, particularly because of the watchful interest of neighboring bishops, always ready to inform the center about unusual developments and dangers. In spite of the limited size of the country and of this facility of communication with the center, we have heard it repeated over and over again that there existed, paradoxically, difficulty for the Italian bishops to meet, because of their number and distance from one another. If this difficulty existed, it all but disappeared when not only 400 Italian bishops, but six times as many bishops from all over the world got together in Rome. The difficulties put forward to prove that the Italian bishops could not meet appeared all but imaginary, once the Council got under way.

At the Council, the Italian bishops confronted one another for the first time in a century. They were unprepared for this meeting as they were for the meeting with the rest of the bishops of the world, and for the Council in general. The majority of them had the outmoded concept of a rubber-stamp Council, on the lines of the Roman Synod. Few of them anticipated the developments that followed. The first session "took them by surprise," in utter disorganization, "masters of eloquence, but devoid of any parliamentary know-how." "We were prepared to *assist* at the Council *not to participate in it,*" said a prominent Italian bishop. "We thought that they would read us some decrees and ask us to vote on them." "We were badly disorganized, a striking contrast to many foreign episcopates," said another bishop. An Italian bishop noted that the choice by election of the chairman of the conference would respond better to the needs of the Church in Italy. But, he was quick to indicate, this procedure would only sharpen the north-south feud that plagues most Italian problems, extending it to the episcopate too. This is because, should an election for the chairman of the Italian Episcopal Conference be held, it can be assumed that the one elected would be a southern cardinal or bishop since the southerners represent a larger number of bishops than the northerners. This is a paradoxical but factual situation: the fragmentation of the central and southern part of Italy into a fantastic number of minute dioceses, sometimes with fewer faithful than some of the largest parishes in big dioceses, boosts the number of southern Italian bishops beyond a significant proportion to the Catholic population which they represent, or to the role which the dioceses of this region have played in the Church during the last decades. The south does not have the intense and organized Catholic Action Movement found in the north, nor is Church participation and membership in general as meaningful and active. But historically the south is fragmented into over a hundred dioceses, and for each of these there must be a bishop. This particular case invites a more general consideration of the representativeness of the Church at the Council through the bishops.

The problem is a very serious one, considering that the final outcome of the Council's work will not be measured by the number and tone of speeches heard in the hall, but by the issues voted upon and the number of votes cast in favor of one or the other alternative. A statistical table of the distribution of Conciliar Fathers by nationalities in the documentation published by INA[2] presents a comparison of the percentage which the bishops of each country represent

2. *Il primo periodo del Concilio Vaticano II,* Istituto Nazionale Assicurazioni (INA), Rome, 1963, p. 87 ff.

to the total number of bishops, correlated to the percentage which their flock represents to the total Catholic population. We have chosen some of the extreme cases for illustration.

Table II: National and World Proportion of Bishops to Catholic Population for Selected Countries

COUNTRY OR AREA	BISHOPS	% OF TOTAL NUMBER OF BISHOPS	% OF WORLD CATHOLIC POPULATION WHICH THEY REPRESENT
Asia (excluding the Arab countries)....	256	9.53	6.14
Europe (excluding the Communist Bloc)..	849	31.60	33.70
Africa (excluding the Arab countries)....	250	9.30	4.08
Latin America.......	601	22.33	35.53
Brazil..............	194	7.22	12.21
Mexico.............	61	2.27	6.02
Philippines..........	48	1.79	4.07
India..............	77	2.87	1.10
Canada.............	96	3.57	1.35
France.............	163	6.07	7.06
Germany (Western)..	58	2.16	4.85
Ireland.............	31	1.15	0.60
Italy..............	344	12.80	8.99
Spain..............	94	3.50	5.68

The U.S.A. appears to enjoy a fairly balanced ratio between the number of its bishops and the Catholic population they represent. The difference could be said to be quite tolerable for the large percentage which U.S. bishops and U.S. Catholics represent on world totals, and is strikingly close to that of Australia.

Of these areas with extreme differences between the percentage of world Catholics and the percentage of bishops to represent them at the Council, the Catholics of Canada, Africa, Asia, Ireland, and Italy are heavily "over-represented," while those of all other areas are "under-represented." The factors that account for the discrepancies are multiple, and vary considerably from country to country. The over-representation for Canada, Africa, and Asia can be explained to a great extent by the spread of a limited number of Catholics over a very large territory. In the case of Ireland and Italy, this reason does not apply.

These considerations are given here as a corroborative argument in favor of the urgency to reconsider and redefine diocesan boundaries for certain areas of the Church, a problem already touched upon during the Second Session, by describing one particular implication of the disfunctionality of the size of the dioceses in one particular region. If any significance at all is to be given to the results of the *voting* at the Council, it is its function as numerical indicators of the mind of the whole Church, in her world-wide dimension, through the representativeness of the bishops. True, this is no parliamentarian system, and representativeness is to be taken in a wide connotation, apart from the fact that the ultimate decision rests with the pope. Yet, if a bishop's vote is to be a real consultation with the whole Church, it stands to reason that care should be taken so that the consultation may discover the actual distribution of the various attitudes among the Catholic community, and not misrepresent factual conditions instead, by giving undue advantage to a group or groups.

Under the pressure of competition with other conferences, the Italians tried to organize themselves. They too held weekly meetings: this was a revelation to them. For the first time they were together and could discuss their problems, as members of the Italian episcopate. But soon it was evident that more would be needed before the Italian conference could reach the efficiency of other conferences. Said one bishop: "We met weekly; attendance was fair, but the meetings reflected the hierarchical structure of the CEI. There was little discussion and effective participation." "We never had the satisfaction of seeing all the Italian cardinals at the meetings: someone or other was usually absent. The meetings turned out to be a waste of time, with no conversation or dialogue. It is not true that we were told how to vote, and no party line was imposed. But there has been a commandeering attitude, and many issues have been handled roughly. An atmosphere of diffidence and division has plagued us." And another bishop said: "The Italian bishops have been conspicuous for their absenteeism from the Council hall and from the meetings. This is the reason why some hard fought battles were lost." Another bishop in a more optimistic vein said: "Our meetings have had a positive effect. We could have this experience only because of the Council. There had been very little collective action by the episcopate in Italy. Our experience in collaboration has been slow, and the need little felt because of the presence of the papacy and because of our large number."

On no occasion during the two sessions was the Italian episcopate able to present a common front or to get the endorsement of all the Italian bishops, with regard to any of the conciliar issues. The few times when Cardinal Siri was delegated to present the position agreed upon, the intervention was carefully worded in the name of "fere omnes," [almost all], a convenient Latin expression that took into account the "dissidents," who might have been more numerous than at first apparent.

But, in itself, this was a significant achievement. Some bishops noted that there were too many chiefs in the conference and that the real problem of the conference turned out to be a leadership crisis after all. The fruits of the meetings, however, cannot be discounted. Little by little, the Italian bishops are seeing their own situation more clearly and trying to come up to the expectations people hold of them.

Our second case study is that of the American Episcopal Conference. Organized in 1919, it comprises two entities: the NCWC and the annual meetings of the bishops. The distinction helps maintain the character of the conference: a national common forum of the episcopate of the U.S.A. with a full guarantee of the autonomy of the individual bishops. It is undeniable that the conference has performed great services and has given national unity to the Catholic Church in the U.S.A. It did not, however, obtain national uniformity in various practices, precisely because of the voluntary character of its membership. In matters affecting the Church, the conference performed a coordinating function among U.S. bishops before the Council by fostering communication among them.

The announcement of a council, however, found the American bishops unprepared for a group response to the event. First of all, they did not anticipate such doctrinal discussion as developed in the Council; they were preoccupied with administrative problems mainly. When suggestions were requested for the Council's agenda, the U.S. bishops did not give any collective response, but gave exclusively individual replies. Although not many other hierarchies gave collective suggestions, the American bishops did meet, and prepared themselves for the Council as a group. But in spite of the frequent meetings among themselves, the U.S. bishops were still following an individualistic line of interest. An American bishop noted that the last time the U.S. bishops gathered to discuss doctrinal matters was at the Third Plenary Council in Baltimore (1884). Like the Italian bishops, the U.S. bishops used to think of their dioceses as directly and immediately linked with Rome, although for good works and for administration there exists an efficacious cooperation among them. But this is a far cry from the image of the Catholic Church in America as a monolithic structure. Each diocese has a different historical background, many dioceses have been established prior to the emergence of federal experience and sentiment. It has brought about a strong identification between the bishops, their dioceses, and the states in which they reside, that overshadows the common American dimension, because the temporal administration of the various dioceses and churches is governed by state not by federal laws.

Up to their arrival in Rome, U.S. bishops reacted individualistically. While in Rome, observing other national conferences meet as distinct groups, some U.S. bishops were at first scandalized. But soon it became evident that corporate identity, distinctively American, was imperative to the U.S. episcopate; and that Catholicism, in its American form, had a definite contribution to make. It was not that easy, though. The proposal was discussed as to whether to hold the annual meeting of the Conference in Rome. Not everyone was in favor of the proposal. A compromise was finally reached, however, by agreeing to hold the meeting in Rome but to refrain from having it publicized by the press.

When the proposal was made at this same meeting that the U.S. bishops should meet periodically during the Council, there was much dissension and disagreement. The proposal was shelved. The compromise solution was to organize committees parallel to those of the Council, as tentative attempts at communication.

After the completion of the first session during the spring of 1963, a gathering of U.S. bishops was suggested, in order to keep them up to date. The suggestion was rejected, but an "informal" gathering was organized in Chicago in August, 1963. There was almost plenary attendance in spite of its informal and free basis. There was free and spontaneous expression of opinion. And the group came out with a pronouncement on racial justice. By now, the stage was set for a regular communication process. During the second session, the U.S. bishops held weekly meetings and made a genuine effort to contribute to the Council in the intellectual sphere. Finally, the question arose as to whether the U.S. bishops should intervene as a group in the discussion. Once again, the expression "in the name of all the American bishops" sounded improper and dangerous, and consequently there was no total representation. On a few occasions, however, some American bishops spoke in the name of a large number of U.S. bishops, as when Bishop Robert Tracy spoke in the name of 147 of them.

Behind these hesitations and cautions, there lies the necessary ambivalence of the NCWC, with its need to serve as a channel of communication and cooperation for the American bishops without detracting from their autonomy and individual initiative. On the other hand, the fear of being labeled with the mark of "Americanism," the traumatic word which time has emptied of much of its original content but which still conveys the idea of cultural separation, paralyzes energies and stifles initiative. With the organization of the American Press Panel and the participation in it of several U.S. bishops, a great step forward in the development of the U.S. conference as a distinctive unit was made. An American bishop said very openly: "I am dissatisfied with the image we have created about the U.S. bishops. It is the fault of our weak organization. The French and German bishops came to the Council knowing what they wanted, well-prepared, even to the extent of having substitute schemes ready. The U.S. bishops were not prepared. They adopted a wait-and-see attitude. Finally, they began to stir and work behind the scenes. They still believe that it suffices only to listen and to vote. But while we think that it is a waste of time to speak, the Germans and others tell us they are waiting to hear our opinions voiced. We must be better prepared for the next session." However, all problems are not ended for the U.S. Episcopal Conference. The schema on "Bishops and the Government of Dioceses" has caused during the second session considerable preoccupation among American bishops. As of the present, the NCWC has no juridical power over its members, but works as a voluntary association. This explains its failure, on particular occasions, to come out with uniform regulations for the whole country as in the laws of fast and abstinence, which vary considerably throughout the U.S.A. Whether some binding force should be given to the decisions of the conference remains to be seen. To complicate matters, a juridical power granted to the conference would entail a change in the role of the auxiliaries in America. As soon as a bishop is consecrated, he is voted into the conference. If binding decision should be given to the conference, his would be a valid vote. This would affect the balance of power among bishops to the manifest advantage of larger dioceses, where auxiliaries are usually found. However, there is a wide recognition of the need to bring the conference up-to-date, and to make the necessary changes, especially in view of its long history and of changed conditions in the country.

It is convenient to add here a few considerations regarding U.S. episcopal relations to other conferences. From our graph (see page 70) it appears that the U.S. bishops did not appoint any official representatives to other episcopal conferences while in Rome. The links with other conferences were informal and on a personal level. Three episcopal conferences from mission countries did appoint official representatives to the meetings of the American hierarchy. Apart from this, there was no evidence that U.S. bishops, *as a conference,* had been close to the center of the communication network in the Council. They rather appear to have been marginal, as a group, and this in spite of the expectations of bishops from other countries.

Prior to the Council there was little, if any, communication among the various episcopal conferences of the world. It was predictable that a sharp increase in the exchange of contacts and views would take place at the Council. The question was what direction the new avenues of thought would take, and what modality.

Because several conferences had weekly meetings, the exchange of observers at these meetings was the first official link between conferences. Conferences with a larger number of bishops had a solid advantage over the smaller ones in this connection. Some of them exploited the situation excellently, as did, for instance, the Spanish conference, by appointing one or two delegates to attend the meetings of other conferences and to report to them their observations. The amount of information and widening of horizons thus gained is beyond measurement. But not all conferences made use of this method. Some did not bother to know officially what other groups of bishops were doing, as for instance the U.S. conference. Still others, like the Italians, after going to the trouble of appointing official delegates to several conferences, never took steps to get them to report and to share their knowledge and impressions of the groups observed.

We may now map out in sociographic form the "official" exchange of delegations among conferences, and the graph under discussion is a very telling page of cultural and national interaction. The calculations for this sociogram were

based on the responses to the question as to whether a conference had "official links" with any other conferences; that
is, whether they sent representatives to participate in, or
to observe the meetings of other conferences. From the
answers, we can design the graph of "sent" or "received"
"official" liaisons so as to make the various trends easily
evident.

France is by far the star of the system, having received
thirteen observers and having sent her own observers to
only two other conferences in reciprocal relation. Italy
follows with eight delegations received and three sent. Next
is Germany with six delegations received and three sent.
England received six delegations and sent none.

On the whole, the Western European conferences received twenty-nine delegations of observing bishops from
non-European conferences, while they sent out but seven
delegations to non-Western European conferences, most of
these being Spanish bishops.

The balance between input and output is heavily in favor
of countries in which the Church is firmly established, while
the African and the Asian bishops looked up to the traditionally Catholic countries for inspiration, knowledge and
guidance. More encouraging is the position of the Latin
American countries. Most of their official relations with
other episcopal groups were channeled through the CE-
LAM, but, in the majority of cases, several conferences
sent observers to the Latin American meetings, while it
seems there were but two official observers sent from Argentina to Germany and to France. From the chart, one can
easily gauge the flow of communication, at the official level,
and the distribution of its intensity. We must note that this
represents only the *official* contacts among conferences, a
fractional aspect of the total process of communication.

The *total* interaction process would add up to substantially different results, but this chart gives us a good indicator of the official and conscious interest and expectation which various conferences had about other episcopal groups.

Table III: Distribution of Officially Appointed Contact-Men between Various Episcopal Conferences

COUNTRIES	NO. OF CONFS. FROM WHICH OBSERVERS WERE RECEIVED	NO. OF CONFS. TO WHICH OBSERVERS WERE SENT	RATIO BETWEEN OBSERVERS RECEIVED AND SENT	TOTAL NUMBER OF "CONTACTS"
France	13	2	6.5	15
England	6	0	6.0	6
Holland	3	0	3.0	3
Italy	8	3	2.7	11
Germany	6	3	2.0	9
Ireland	2	3	0.66	5
Spain	5	9	0.55	14
Belgium	0	1	—	1
Western Europe & other Countries	29	7	4.1	36
United States	3	0	3.0	3
Canada	2	0	2.0	2
Australia	2	4	0.5	6
Asian Countries & Non-Asn. Cnts.	0	16	—	16
African Countries & Non-African Countries	1	8	0.12	9
Latin-Am. Countries & Non-Lat. Am. Cnts.	7	2	3.5	9
English Speaking Countries & others	10	4	2.5	14
East. European Countries & others	1	3	0.33	4

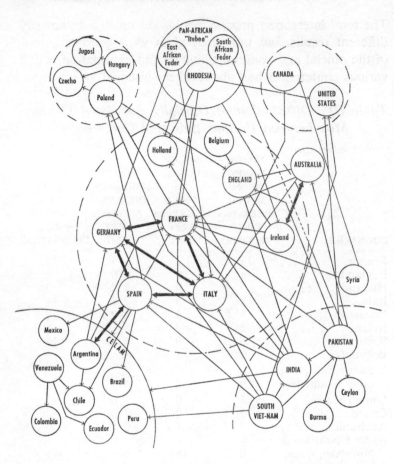

Sociogram of official "exchanges" between Episcopal Conferences. Arrows indicate to which conference observers were sent and by whom. Heavy line indicates mutual exchange of observers.

V

Individual Contacts
and Group Dynamics

Informal Groups

The common joke among Council Fathers had it that two
councils were going on at the same time: Vatican II and
"Lateranense VI," the latter being the individual and group
meetings that went on in the side aisles of St. Peter's (the
"Ali Laterali") while the official sessions took place. And
indeed there were two very distinct phases in the proceed-
ings of a typical conciliar day: the official and well-struc-
tured morning sessions, in an atmosphere of high concentration of persons and contacts, strongly formalized; and
the afternoon activities, mostly informal, in groups of small
and manageable dimensions, at the individual and personal
level, in which one could follow private liking.

Part of this informal structure of communication took
place in a semi-organized way, unofficial, but none the less
deeply efficacious. We could identify four informal groups
of bishops, who met regularly, in different places, to discuss
and exchange viewpoints and to map out strategies for the
general sessions and for confrontation with Church problems in general.

Under the leadership of the Argentinian bishops, one
group met at the Caesar Augustus hotel with the participa-

71

tion of the bishops of Uraguay, Paraguay, Chile, Ecuador, Colombia and Mexico. But only very little information could be gathered about these meetings, as also was true of another similar group which met periodically at the Americana Hotel. Here the participants were once again from Latin American countries, like Venezuela, Paraguay, Ecuador, and Bolivia, with fifty to sixty bishops participating.

By far the most important and diversified informal gathering was the one organized by the Brazilian bishops at the Domus Mariae. Its initial membership consisted of representatives of five episcopal conferences, but rapidly it expanded and by the end of the Second Session it had representatives from well over twenty episcopal conferences from all over the world. The participants were, generally, bishops who occupied central positions in their own conferences, such as chairman or secretary, and it was readily discernible that they shared, within limits, a common forward-looking point of view. The countries identified as participants were: France, Germany, Brazil, Chile, Australia, England, India, Cameroon, Tanganyika, Rhodesia, Ecuador, the Philippines, Congo (Leo), Canada, Japan, Spain, the U.S.A. and Italy. Most Latin American countries were indirectly represented by the presence of high ranking officers of the CELAM. Among the animating forces of this group, which met regularly every Friday, was Archbishop Helder Camara, a small, affable, smiling man, who beguiled the unsuspecting observers with his simplicity, which screened off one of the most outstanding organizers of the whole Catholic episcopate.

Among these participants at the Domus Mariae, there reigned at the meetings the highest enthusiasm and genuine interest. More important still, according to their statements, several key issues and resolutions of the Council were pre-

pared and matured at these meetings. Because the participants held, in most cases, strategic power positions, they
could influence a large number of bishops of their episcopates. Consequently, the group acted as a sounding-board
for new ideas, and as a promoter for advanced positions.

The Domus Mariae group did not meet with the approval
of a small number of bishops from Latin American and
Latin European countries. Unwilling to go along with the
more progressive group, they considered themselves as
"dissidents," in their own joking language, and organized
informal meetings of their own where they could feel enough
group-support for their viewpoints as well. Available information concerning this group was even more scanty:
only indirectly could allusions to its activities be gathered.
It appears that the group was organized at the suggestion of
a small number of Brazilian bishops, together with some
other Latin American bishops who felt isolated and out-of-
step with the rather progressive majority of their own episcopates. They requested the use of a hall near Piazza St.
Ufficio ostensibly "for the use of a CELAM group." Their
meetings were not publicized at all. Even the rector of the
"locale" where the meetings were being held remained in
ignorance of the goings-on there. Attendance was limited
to less than thirty participants, among whom there were
prominent Italian prelates who in their interventions in the
Council Hall had clearly characterized themselves as being
of rather conservative leaning. One Latin American bishop
confessed: "I was invited to join an international group of
those who are more conservative (he smiled), but I did not
accept because I am too busy writing the constitutions of
a women's congregation which I am erecting in my diocese."
Said another bishop: "We met every Tuesday, at Santa
Monica. This was the meeting of the 'dissidents' who felt
that they could not go along with the majority in their

episcopal conferences. There were Italians, some Brazilians, Mexicans, Argentinians, and Portuguese. I was invited to go, but I still don't understand why."

It goes without saying that in their own right these informal groups performed a valuable function in the total interaction process of the Council. Still, it is difficult to dispel a feeling of puzzlement due to the fact that they acted under such circumstances; few were aware of the existence of these groups. The atmosphere of secrecy extended from the Council Hall to these informal meetings, though the restrictions of formal procedures and the feeling of awe unavoidable with the general assembly were absent.

The central significance of such a smaller group formation is manifold. First, it calls attention to the need for a sizeable limitation of group membership, where participation is easier and more rewarding. This represents a reaction to the enormous general sessions in the Council Hall. Second, it afforded the more capable leaders extensive scope to channel and to exploit their greater energies in the direction of more control and greater involvement in the Council. Third, it provided identification and support, because the members of the groups were selectively homogeneous, and held approximately a similar range of attitudes. For this third factor, these groups contributed to a sustained and deeper penetration of issues by stalling the too-rapid disintegration of whichever group held a minority position. In the surge of a tangible majority, it was an easy temptation that prompted those who disagreed with it to fade away into inconspicuousness. Strengthened by the realization that other bishops thought similarly, they rendered a valuable service in upholding the theoretical and practical positions which they thought more appropriate. It became forcefully necessary for the majority to deepen and to further clarify its own positions, and to carry the burden of exhaustively legitimizing it in differentiation from that held by the minority.

Group Spokesmen

From the first days of the first session, yet another interesting phenomenon could be observed in the Council Hall, which may be considered particularly significant as an indicator of group cohesion and homogeneity. The speakers at the Council were primarily intended to represent personal convictions and ideas, each bishop speaking as an official "doctor" in the Church and having the right to one vote. Spontaneously, and without any suggestion from the directing body, however, several episcopal groups soon delegated, on various occasions, one or another bishop to speak in the name of them all. This simplified interventions, cut down the discussion time and, above all, threw behind the spokesman the weight of an entire episcopate.

During the first session, seven speakers addressed the Council in the name of the entire African episcopate, more than 250 strong, a feature that appears incredible at first, if one considers the variety of nations, races, and cultures that this number represents. This was the most outstanding case. It would be repeated on two more occasions during the Second Session too.

A similar common voice was heard for the bishops of Japan, the Philippines, Holland, Poland, France, and from Latin America's Chile, Argentina, Venezuela, Mexico, and Colombia. Only once did an American bishop speak "in the name of various bishops," and yet another "in the name of a large number of American bishops."

At the Second Session, more hierarchies threw their weight as a body behind a single bishop, a propos of various issues. The Polish, Dutch, Venezuelan, and African episcopates repeated the performance of the First Session, but they were joined by newcomers like Ecuador, Bolivia, Thailand, Laos, Indonesia, Czechoslovakia, England and Wales, Switzerland, and, most strikingly, Brazil. The Brazilian and the African groups scored the most frequent instances of group interventions, the Brazilians often specifying the number of bishops in whose name the intervention was made, (153, 133, 110, 121, 60), while the Africans spoke for area groupings like South Africa and Rhodesia, North Africa, and the Rwanda episcopal conference.

The Indonesian and the Polish bishops had a persistent liking for delegating one bishop to speak for all. Yet even after such frequently-heard group interventions, many of the largest and most important episcopal groups could never muster the totality of consensus needed to speak in the name of all their bishops.

Archbishop Florit of Italy could muster "fifty followers and a few other bishops" on one occasion, Cardinal Siri once made a proposal in the name of *"fere omnes"* [almost all] the Italian bishops, which was the closest this group came to consensus on one issue. All the other Italians spoke for themselves, or for a handful of adherents or friends. The U.S.A. could muster a maximum strength of 147 bishops who delegated Bishop Tracy as spokesman, and on another occasion 120 bishops, or "several other bishops." The total number of American bishops is given at 236, but not all of them were present at the Council. In addition, it appears that even the German bishops did not choose to present a unified front on purely national lines. Twice the Germans appointed a spokesman, once to represent sixty-seven German and Austrian bishops, and another time to represent seventy-nine German and Scandinavian bishops, while on at least one occasion Archbishop John C. Heenan spoke in the name of the hierarchy of England and Wales.

The other episcopates stayed even further away from

total consensus. Canada managed to get forty-five bishops together once, Spain sixty, India only "several" bishops represented by Bishop Fernandes, China only fifteen, and Yugoslavia and Ireland "several" bishops. Some episcopal groups may have signified virtual consensus on some occasions, but they did not care to make it explicit and throw their full weight, as a body, behind their spokesman.

We shall see in the course of this study that one of the most frequently heard suggestions in order to simplify and expedite the work of the assembly was that only group spokesmen be allowed to intervene; this has been partially achieved already, spontaneously, during the past sessions. It goes to prove that it can be adopted as a method in future sessions, provided that the various episcopates reach the minimum level of consensus of opinion required and provided that the necessary mechanism to bring about this consensus is available.

Formal Groups: The Commissions

More than half of the bishops interviewed were members of commissions, and some of them had belonged to some preparatory commission as well. The ten commissions numbered twenty-five members each, thus including a total of 250 members. Our respondents, therefore, constituted over 14% of the commissions, while representing only 3.5% of the total number of bishops. Almost unanimously they said that they liked and enjoyed working on the commissions. It had been a worthwhile experience in their lives and had more than compensated for the trouble of having to come to Rome so frequently. One particular bishop, in a central position, had made twenty-two trips from his native Spain to Rome, in connection with the Council.

But not all agreed that the work done in the commission

was useful. Said one bishop: "I worked on the theological commission and did not like it. It was interesting for the contacts I made with other bishops and theologians, but there was too much politics involved, in addition to applied forces and pressures. Because he knows that we [the more progressive type of bishops, that is] are in the majority, our president blocks decisions. We waste whole hours just discussing and politicking. It is like a chess board game. The biggest mistake of Pope John was to have placed the commissions under the Curia." Others equally familiar with the workings of the commission hinted strongly that a counter-tactic of persevering patience early set in and in the long haul turned the dilatory procedures of the commission leadership into an advantage to progressive positions.

The most frequent complaint was that much work done in the commissions was futile, and could be used only for the commission for the revision of Canon Law. "I did not like working on the commissions," said another bishop, "because of the lack of a sense of reality in them. The whole thing was too theoretical, juridical, and clerical, out of touch with basic problems of the Church, outmoded in economic and social aspects. I was deeply disturbed to find us [members of the commission on the lay apostolate] discussing these problems without a single lay observer, advisor, or consultant present. This is the reason why out of such voluminous work very little has been utilized and so much has been scrapped." This complaint of a massive accumulation of material, only part of which was or could ever be used at the Council, was among the most frequently heard grievances.

Less frequently mentioned but more negative in nature were references to the existence of some degree of conflict between the commissions and the parallel congregations.

In the words of one rather conservative bishop: "I would not anticipate much collaboration from the Roman congregations, of course. There is a high probability of conflict because of the difference in viewpoints. I would have liked to have worked under another head other than that of the congregation. Although the congregations collaborated with us, the issues were faced from different perspectives. The schemata are not the work of the congregations, but of the commissions. Those who are at the congregations know more about the points in question." And another bishop: "The juridical problems were very well studied, but there was no way of including the pastoral implications of the work they were doing. The bishops on the other hand were afraid of proposing points that seemed to go beyond the province of the commission." One African bishop stated that he was under the impression that his "commission was being suffocated by the interference of the corresponding Curial section."

On one point all the members of the various commissions agreed. This was that working on the commissions had given them an excellent opportunity for knowing more intimately a larger group of important bishops of the Church. As each commission numbered twenty-five members, it was well within the optimum limits for a small-sized group to obtain maximum group interaction. The composition of the commissions was varied, and at times included more than a dozen nationalities. Each commission met at various times and with different formalities, but they all contributed substantially to the process of integration among bishops, even when the various members disagreed strongly about basic issues. The bond of having worked together on the same commission kept them united and gave them a sense of group identification with regard to the issues involved.

Table IV: *Patterns of Individual Acquaintances and Friendships between Bishops Made during the Council*

... with Bishops from these countries. Respondent/s from these countries made new acquaintances ...	FRANCE	GERMANY	SPAIN	ITALY	BELGIUM	ENGLAND	HOLLAND	SWITZERLAND	AUSTRIA	IRELAND	PORTUGAL	YUGOSLAVIA	HUNGARY	CZECHOSLOVAKIA
FRANCE		2	2	1	1	1		1				1		
GERMANY	1			1			1							
SPAIN		1							1					
ITALY	3	2	1			1		1	1		1		1	
BELGIUM	1		1	1		1								
ENGLAND			1											
IRELAND							1							
POLAND	1	1			1							1		1
YUGOSLAVIA		1		1										
U. S. A.	3	2		1		2				1				
CANADA	1													
BRAZIL	1	2	1		1			1	1			1		1
ARGENTINA	1	1						1	1	1				
PANAMA	1	1	1	1	1									
VENEZUELA			1	1										
BOLIVIA	1		1											
CHILE	1	1												
ECUADOR			1		1									
COLOMBIA					1									
MEXICO	1													
PARAGUAY		1												
INDIA	1	2	1	1	1	1	1							
INDONESIA		1				1								
JAPAN	1	1												
PHILIPPINES			1											
VIET-NAM	1													
MADAGASCAR	1													
RHODESIA		1	1	1										
TANGANYIKA		1												
SOUTH AFRICA	1		1											
CONGO	1					1								
TOTAL	22	21	14	10	9	6	5	4	2	2	1	2	2	1

N.B.: Countries in left hand columns represent *part* of our sample. Bishops from these countries made *new* acquaintances among bishops from countries in the upper row. The total at the bottom line therefore represents an approximate indicator of the degree to which bishops of that particular group were "in demand" as new acquaintances and friends. Indexes on the right-

Respondent/s belonging to countries in left hand column made new acquaintances among Bishops from countries in upper row

U. S. A.	Canada	Australia	New Zealand	Latin America	Brazil	Mexico	Asian Bishops	India	Indonesia	Pakistan	Philippines	African Bishops	Oriental Bishops	Missionary Bishops	English Speaking Bishops	Index
2	2			1								1				5
1				1												5
				1												3
1				3	1	1						2	1	1		3
		1	1	1				1	1			1				9
1								1		1		1				3
1															1	4
1												1				7
1																3
	1	1		1			1					1			1	3.5
				1												2
1	1			1				1				1				4.7
				1												3
				1												6
1				1							1	1				6
1				1								1		1		5
				1				1								4
				1	1											4
																2
																1
																1
1		1		2			1					1			2	3.7
	1													1		4
													1			2
				1												3
																2
												1				2
1	1			1												3
				1			1									3
																2
														1		3
13	**6**	**3**	**1**	**21**	**2**	**1**	**3**	**4**	**1**	**1**	**1**	**12**	**2**	**4**	**4**	

hand final column may be taken as *approximate* indicators of "openness" or "outgoing capability" of the *respondents* belonging to the respective countries, during the council. The index was obtained by dividing the number of *New* acquaintances by the number of respondents, for each country. A little over 10% of the respondents declined to answer the question.

Personal Contacts: Individual Level

All the known laws and regularities governing interaction between individuals in a group could receive confirmation and added illustration from the example of the contacts that took place among the 2300 bishops in Rome. It is a well-known fact that when an idea or a proposal is identified with the person who supports or suggests it, our attitude towards it assumes a different trend than it would had we conceived of the idea in purely abstract form. Let us note, too, that the clusters of groups of bishops did not and could not follow exclusively national or cultural lines. Many other facts came into play to pattern the network of relationships among bishops more in the form of a mesh, intricately interwoven along unsuspected lines.

Three factors are pertinent to our case: 1) the language areas to which the bishops belonged; 2) the school-mate links; and 3) the position occupied and the international experience already possessed.

The allegiance of bishops in heterogeneous episcopates was a complex, and at times conflicting, set of "belongings." Few episcopates were homogeneous. The mission countries as well as many Latin American countries numbered among their ranks bishops belonging to several nationalities. This situation made them excellent go-between linking groups of bishops which otherwise would have had little contacts. Thus, for example, the common German language brought together bishops from Germany, Austria, Switzerland, and many Latin Americans, especially from Brazil and Argentina. The French brought together bishops from France, North Africa, parts of Canada, and Southeast Asia. Dutch brought together bishops from Holland and Indonesia. Spanish was the factor that brought together bishops from Central and South America and from Spain. Portuguese, however, failed to act as link between Brazilians and Portuguese bishops, as we have seen.

Many bishops were individually linked across national lines through their long-time friendships with bishops who had studied with them at Roman colleges. This was a particularly interesting situation because it followed no other line but historical happenstance. In some cases this represented rather interesting combinations, as the one where an Italian cardinal had been a theology professor to one of the most prominent Italian bishops at the Council, who in turn had been professor to a yet younger Italian bishop. This three-academic-generations cluster showed remarkable homogeneity in their strongly conservative points of view, while clearly remaining distinct personalities. Once again, to help us chart the patterns of personal contacts developed during the Council, each respondent was asked to indicate among which group he had made the most acquaintances and friends during the Council—the pattern parallels to a great extent the previous one illustrating the official contacts and representatives among Conferences. The French group once again scores the highest number: twenty-two non-French bishops said that they were acquainted and made new friends among the French episcopate. Germany follows with twenty-one, then Spain with fourteen, the U.S. with thirteen, Italy with ten, Belgium with nine, England with six, Canada with six, Holland with five, Switzerland with four, Australia with three, and Austria with two. The interest in pursuing new acquaintances and friendships seems to have been concentrated on the Western European countries more intensely than was apparent on the previous chart of the official representations. Of the non-European countries, only bishops from India were mentioned four times. The Latin American bishops were mentioned fourteen times *"en bloque"* by non-Latin Americans, and seven times by Latin Americans. Other national groups were mentioned occasionally. If any meaning can be read into these figures, it once again points to

the predominant role which the Western European bishops
played, and the amount of interest and attention they received from the rest of the world.

In contrast with the former chart, the U.S. and Canadian
bishops this time rank highest. This indicates that there
has been a large degree of interest on the part of non-
Americans for the North Americans, which interest was
not necessarily reciprocated.

With particular reference to U.S. bishops, the phenomenon has various possible explanations. For one, few U.S.
bishops have the knowledge of foreign languages needed
for intense contacts, while on the other hand, several bishops
from other parts of the world speak English. Furthermore,
the U.S. bishops felt rather self-sufficient, and the urge to
contact, discuss with, and question bishops from other
countries was secondary to the major concern: to play their
role at the Council. More decisive still was the awareness of
a calculated risk one runs in approaching a bishop from
the developing areas of the world. Correctly or not, many
U.S. bishops feared that their contacts with missionary
bishops or Latin American bishops would sooner or later
become the occasion for requests and financial involvement
in aid to that country. How real this difficulty was is proved
by the fact that an official of the NCWC was in Rome during the Second Session with the specific purpose to get
together, in small and controllable groups, U.S. and Latin
American bishops under such circumstances where the
U.S. bishops would not be bothered with requests for financial help.

It was striking to note that the German bishops did not
seem to be concerned by similar difficulties, although in the
past decade their financial help to churches in developing
countries, especially in Latin America, has been propor-
tionately equal, if not greater, than that of the American
community.

A Canadian bishop stated plainly: "As for other countries, I know very well those bishops who have come to me to ask for money, about a hundred of them from all over the world . . ." And yet another North American bishop, commenting upon the number of new acquaintances made during the Council said: ". . . at the end of the Council, the American bishops will be sending five times as many Christmas cards, as they used to do before. U.S. bishops have become intensely aware of the bishops of other countries and have gained a deeper knowledge of them . . . as for me, I discovered Catholic Africa at this Council and was highly impressed by the work done by the European missionaries in that continent. . . ." The opportunity offered to the bishops was abundantly used by the majority, though not by all. Some bishops were of necessity compelled to play a marginal role, either because of health or lack of time, or because, as one prelate commented, "I am not very good at making acquaintances and meeting people." Another bishop candidly stated: "I had no time and was not interested in meeting many bishops. Of those whom I met, I remember the faces, but don't know their names."

One of the preliminary questions asked was whether the respondents knew and were acquainted with all the bishops of their own country before the Council. As was to be expected, the bishops belonging to smaller episcopates unanimously agreed that they knew all the bishops of their country. But this was not the case with larger episcopates such as the Italian, the U.S., the French, the Canadian, the Brazilian, and to some extent the Indian. In such instances, only a few claimed to know all the other bishops in their respective hierarchies.

They were also asked whether the Council had helped them to come to know all the bishops of their country. The answer was affirmative in all cases except the Italian bishops, who, in spite of the opportunity afforded by the Council, were unable to acquaint themselves with their fellow Italian bishops. On the whole, a significant progress, quantitatively speaking, has been achieved among a large number of episcopates, and the Council has served the function of creating the conditions whereby at least the bishops of the same country could know each other. An American bishop had this to say: "At the meetings of the U.S. bishops up until recently, we still had to wear identification badges. I can say now that I know all the 240 American bishops."

In summation, the largest gain from the Council was derived by the French, German, Spanish, Belgian, American and the Central European bishops in general. They succeeded in attaining an outstanding degree of personal popularity and widely shared recognition. The Latin American bishops gained recognition as a group, rather than as individual personalities. The African and Asiatic group, the bishops of the Iron Curtain countries and the Latin American bishops from smaller nations, occupied a marginal position in terms of the personal, informal, and individual interest of the participant bishops. An Indian bishop made an excellent analysis of the situation: "Although on the surface there is an apparent willingness to meet, still there is a large number of bishops who are not willing to meet their brothers in the episcopate. They are not interested. There still exists a ghetto mentality that needs to be eliminated. I did not find the warmth and interest that I had anticipated." It may seem that this statement, could be attributed to the hurt feelings of the respondent as an individual. But the sociometric chart gave support to his observation. It makes it all the more imperative to examine the unused potentiality of the Council for providing an atmosphere of true Christian understanding and love, and a step towards the practice of "collegiality."

VI

When Silence Speaks
More Than Words

The Periti

In previous councils, a large portion of the discussion and numerous interventions were made by the theologians present there. The procedure was altered fundamentally at the present Council: not once did any *Peritus* or theologian address the Council meeting publicly in St. Peter's. Yet the contribution of *periti* to this council, and the role they played, cannot be sufficiently emphasized. The enquiry focused on two points: 1) what was the distribution of *periti* and of the contacts between bishops and *periti*: 2) how did the bishops see the role of the *periti* at the Council, and what future implications could be concluded?

At the First Session, 280 *periti* participated or were officially appointed. A few more were added at the Second Session. More important than knowing their exact number is the realization that by far the majority of them came from Europe and North America, particularly from Germany, France, Italy, Spain, Belgium, the U.S. and Canada. The *periti* of countries other than the ones mentioned above could be counted on the fingers of one hand. As specialists in particular fields, mostly theology, ethics, canon law and liturgy, they represented the cream of the intellectual resources at the disposal of the Church. It was evident that the use that would be made of these resources was crucial in the total direction and outcome of the Council.

To a large extent, the groups of *periti* were first and foremost at the disposal of the various episcopates to which they were attached or of the individual bishops who had appointed them. In this respect, the episcopal groups from missionary countries of Asia and Africa were at a disadvantage. On the other hand, whether out of genuine willingness to share or with the aim of enlarging one's own area of cultural influence, many of the most important *periti* were placed at least partially at the disposal of all the episcopal groups that cared to make use of them. The engagements for conferences and lectures of such well-known personalities as Congar, Küng, de Lubac, Rahner, Ratzinger, Thils, Philips, et al., were too numerous for them to do full justice to all the invitations received. From this inquiry, it appears that by far the majority of bishops, from all countries, had the opportunity to attend at least some of the conferences given by these outstanding theologians. Several bishops went much further and systematically contacted the best men in the field, to avail themselves of this excellent opportunity for learning.

There were the inevitable exceptions, of course: only two of ten Italian bishops interviewed said they had had any contacts with non-Italian *periti*. The others simply said they did not even try to make use of them, and did not see the need for them. Apart from the peculiarly unique group of the Italian bishops, nearly all the other bishops proved receptive and desirous to contact the *periti*. The reason for the peculiar behavior of the Italian bishops is linked to the

overall attitude taken by the Italian episcopate in their relations with theologians and men of science. The Italian
periti, forming a considerable group and a large percentage
of the total number of *periti*, were "the most conspicuous
for their silence and their absence from tangible contribution." Never did any Italian *peritus* venture to participate
in any of the series of lectures and conferences given to the
bishops at the international level. Apart from lecturing to
the Italian bishops themselves, there was hardly any contribution made by them to the general body of bishops as
a whole. Moreover, even with respect to the Italian episcopate, the collaboration between bishops and *periti* was
almost nonexistent. As some bishops put it: "We Italian
bishops did all the work by ourselves . . . the Italian
periti played a lesser role than foreigners, because the
Italian bishops consider themselves self-sufficient and do not
care to ask for advice and help from *periti*." And a foreign
bishop: "There has been no request on the part of the
Italian bishops for help from their *periti*. They were very
discouraged and remained silent."

A few Italian bishops softened the judgment about their
periti by attributing their behavior to "timidity and shying
away from exhibitionism," or to a lack of organization, or
even to the fact that "the Italian *periti* are balanced men,
with a fine equilibrium in their thinking." This, in the mind
of the respondents, contrasted strongly with the ways and
thinking of foreign *periti*, particularly the Germans and the
French. Consequently, too, foreign *periti* were never invited
to address the Italian episcopal body. Said a very reliable
informant: "We did not feel the need of hearing them. The
Presidential Council of the CEI did not think it fitting to
invite them . . . how could we invite such men as Küng,
de Lubac, Rahner, etc., to talk to us? They lack equilib-

rium . . ." Another Italian bishop, in all simplicity, said: "I approached some non-Italian *periti* . . . but with diffidence."

The most perspicacious among the Italian bishops, however, seem to have realized the need to organize the Italian *periti* on the lines of the French and German group, to request more help and collaboration from them and eventually to formulate ways of making the results of recent studies and research in the religious disciplines accessible to bishops who have neither the time nor the means to keep abreast of theological progress. The more lengthy treatment we have given to the peculiar conditions of the Italian *periti* was called for by the anomalous disproportion between their number and their influence at the Council, and also because of the exceptional role they played (or rather they did not play) at the Council.

In contrast with the Italian situation, the missionary bishops were unable to make use of *periti* they did not have, while clamoring for them. With hardly any theological faculty or institutions of higher learning, and with limited financial power, they were strongly handicapped. The disadvantage was intensified by the fact that the approach and specialization of the majority of *periti* was thoroughly Western, and consequently did not respond to the needs of missionary areas. Said one bishop from Asia: "By and large, the topics raised at the Council referred to the Western countries. When we asked the *periti* *our* questions and *our* problems, they had no answers. They make laws for our regions, too, but without knowing the actual situation there."

Several missionary bishops, however, were very deeply interested and alert to the possibility of a supranational taskforce of *periti,* upon whom they could draw for technical help and guidance, even on a temporary basis. This suggestion was raised several times in the course of the interviews. The bishops from Asia and Africa are looking forward to a theological foreign-aid program, badly needed especially if the resolutions of the Council have to be implemented. They are faced, however, with constant difficulties of men and money: the top experts of the Church are monopolized by the highest institutions and to have them travel to various countries, perhaps in teams, would require a large outlay of funds, and an organization not yet available. Yet there is a crying need for a genuine catholic exchange of this vital resource that is represented by the best theologians and Church scientists, if the whole Church is to raise her standard of religious life.

At a more generic level, with implications for the whole Church, one could find evidence that the Council might have modified somehow the position and role of the "man of science" in the Church. Forty-three bishops from among the respondents expressed appreciation for the dialogue that has developed during the Council, between bishops and *periti*. Nearly all of them agreed that this dialogue represents a modification and an improvement, and should also continue after the Council. But not all were certain that it would take the form of an organized institution so as to make consultation with the *periti* a permanent feature of Church life. Several bishops, however, were fully aware of the crucial importance of this problem, brought to light by the Council. In the words of a Latin American bishop: "I am going to propose that we should give more importance to our *periti*. They have never spoken in the Hall yet . . . but we realize that they are indispensable. Pastoral action must be sustained by a sound theology. And we bishops are not always good theologians. The role of the theologians in the future is going to be very important." Other bishops called the *periti* in technical language the *"organi secundarii magisterii"* and "appendages to the bishops," "the guiding minds of the Council." Yet another stated that "the dialogue between bishops and *periti* was among the best fruits of the Council."

With particular reference to the American situation, one bishop with insight noted that "the American bishops, as a consequence of the Council, will become aware of the presence of theologians and of the role they play in the Church. Some bishops persist in their allergy to these ideas; but there are going to be significant changes in the status of the theologians. Formerly we thought that the '*Ecclesia docens*' implied only the pope and the bishops. Although we made use of the theologians, we considered them merely as seminary professors. Now we see that being a theologian entails a vocation not only for the instruction of young seminarians, but also for the total '*edificatio Ecclesiae*.' That some bishops have begun to understand this, represents nothing less than a first class miracle . . . whether the dialogue is going to continue or not, the bishops, as individuals and as a group, will have greater respect for the *periti*. This might already have existed at the diocesan level. What makes it interesting is that for the first time this is happening at the national level."

Only ten bishops felt that there was nothing new in the relations between bishops and *periti*. They pointed to the fact that the Roman congregations had been using the services of theologians ever since Trent, and that the same holds in many dioceses. One or two bishops objected that there may be dangers in a modification of the status of the theologian: "Let us not forget that the bishop is responsible for the government of the diocese. . . ."

On the whole the general impression can be summarized in the following conclusions: The part played by the *periti* at the Council varied according to the national groups of bishops to which they were attached. The general impression was that the German *periti* did all the work for the German bishops and even prepared their interventions in the Hall. This was not so evident for the French bishops, many of whom appear to have prepared their interventions with little or no consultation with their *periti*. It was almost nil with the Italian bishops, who, generally speaking, ignored their own *periti* (and all the more the foreign ones).

One Belgian bishop stressed particularly the fact that "we prepare our own interventions in the Hall, without outside help." Apart from the difficulty in ascertaining which interventions were the fruit of personal labor and which represented borrowed lucubrations by helpful *periti,* the whole question may present a lopsided view of things. If it is reason for pride that a bishop may prepare his ten minute speech all by himself, it is nonetheless even more useful to the Church if what he says represents the considered opinion of experts in the field, whom he has consulted and in collaboration with whom he has succeeded in achieving a new view of the problem.

In keeping with the basic catholic interest of the Church, it appears imperative that the availability of this most crucial resource, i.e., the *periti,* be homogeneously made available to the episcopate and the Church as a whole. When it was suggested that this pattern of collaboration between bishops and *periti* be made into a permanently organized function in the Church, many bishops were taken by surprise, never having thought it to be feasible. But they were equally quick to realize the pressing need for it, as the key factor for creating those conditions whereby a minimum degree of religious literacy can be fostered throughout the Catholic world. Behind this suggestion is the preoccupation concerning the whole process of resocialization of the Catholic masses, if the outcome of the Council is to have any meaning at all. This appears nearly impossible unless the Church can muster a large group of intellectual task-forces, endowed with high mobility and placed at the service of the various episcopates throughout the world, to organize intensified courses of theological and pastoral *aggiornamento* for the clergy, the religious and the faithful.

The Observers

The novelty represented by the presence of the non-Catholic observers at the Council was at the same time the fruit of past developments and the cause of yet new turns in the relations between the Roman Catholic Church and the other Christian bodies. To many bishops the presence of the observers was an eye-opener, at times accepted slowly but inevitably with the forcefulness of a *fait accompli*. The observers were internationally known figures in their respective Churches, but one could not have expected that they be personally known by the Roman Catholic bishops. With the exception of very few bishops, all acknowledged that never before had they met any of the observers. The fortunate ones had met them at international interfaith gatherings or at the local level, living in the same city.

Nearly all the bishops said that they had met personally and immediately at least a few observers during the Council. The most frequent name was the Brothers of Taizé, invariably mentioned with much admiration and affection, and with the implied agreement that they were practically considered Catholics. Even some Italian bishops had met them, although significantly enough, all but one of the Italian bishops stated that they had no contacts with the other observers. One Italian bishop expressed a negative attitude in general, regarding the presence of the observers at the Council. Said he, "There are disadvantages in having the observers in the Hall. Because of their presence, we sense a certain restriction, control, and limitation in our freedom. To us it seems as if this is a Council in the market place [un concilio in piazza] . . ." And he concluded more generally: "In Italy we can expect only trouble from this whole ecumenical movement . . . because here all we have are sects and unfrocked priests at their command."

This, once again, was a very unique attitude and situation, not shared by any other episcopal group, nor even commonly held by all the Italian bishops. The larger group of bishops agreed that in general the presence of the observers at the Council has generated far-reaching changes in the ecumenical problem. Many bishops went a long way to approach and to contact the observers. The Spanish bishops had them officially for dinner, many others invited them privately or called upon them for lectures and discussion, as happened most frequently with Dr. Cullmann. But the immediate contact with the observers in Rome represented a situation altogether different from the ecumenical problem back home. Although most bishops were much aware of the importance and urgency of ecumenism, they gave a second, objective thought to the actuality of it and almost unanimously realized its flabbergasting complexity, for the ecumenical problem takes on basically different nuances and color, in practically every country.

In Italy it is a marginal problem of few isolated sectarian groups, and of passing tourists and NATO soldiers. In France, the problem is felt more intensely in the eastern dioceses, one or two of which have nearly half of the total Protestant population of France. In Germany, the ecumenical movement, of necessity and tradition, reaches its most sophisticated and most promising manifestation, but it is not duplicated in its form and content anywhere else in the world. A bishop noted: "the writings of Father Küng on ecumenism reflect the situation as it obtains in central Europe and the preoccupation with problems alien to other countries." In Ireland, the situation varies in the north and south. In the north, it is a religious issue enmeshed in political consequences of franchise and employment. Al-

though there has been a beginning in the expression of
goodwill, an organized form of dialogue is yet to come.
There is a dichotomy between popular opinions: some see
the need of breaking down the barriers with the separated
brethren while others see the dangers of confusion that
could arise from a misinterpretation of ecumenism. Some
progress has been made in the last few years (e.g., some
common legislation has been worked out), yet it has remained notably slow and of little consequence.

In the United States, there appears to be a great practical
progress, at the level of contacts, interaction, cooperation
in good works and above all, organized groups of dialogue
between Catholics and non-Catholics. But there appears
to be less perception of the theoretical and more profound
universal implications of ecumenism. In Australia, the lack
of world-renowned theologians makes it also difficult to
intensify the dialogue. The situation in the mission countries
of Africa and Asia is altogether different, because here
ecumenism would have to take into account those sects
which represent the most hostile and aggressive section of
non-Catholic christianity. A slackening of the resistance to
the sects would bring about confusion and hesitation among
the Catholic converts who need to be strengthened in their
loyalty and clearly given a strong sense of identification
with the Church and a disidentification with different religious groups. Ecumenism, at some points, appears to be
the very opposite of missionary evangelization, where both
concepts are understood in the antiquated context of neat
denominational distinction and opposition.

Added to this is the fact that Protestant sects still maintain
all their aggressiveness, because they are not participants in
the ecumenical movement of larger Protestant bodies. In
Indonesia, for instance, even the established Protestant
bodies still retain the old-stamp Protestant antagonism to
Catholicism, which they have lost in the mother country.

Even more varied is the situation in Latin America. Here the two trends converge, for the Catholics are confronted with established Protestantism (Lutherans, Presbyterians, etc.) with whom dialogue is possible and actual, and at the same time with aggressive sects with whom no contact is possible. A significant number of Latin American bishops recognized a profound change introduced since the time of Pope John and gave instances of contacts and collaboration with non-Catholics.

In Central America, on the other hand, the problem is not even stated, first because Protestants are represented predominantly by sects, secondly, because the Catholics are not interested. The crucial problem here is quite different. The need is for more Catholics to build a bridge with the modern world and all that it represents, unless the Church is to lag behind as a remnant of the past era. In yet another area, Yugoslavia, and the Communist countries, ecumenism means preoccupation with finding a way of communication with atheists.

The press has given a relevance out of proportion to the position of Protestants in Spain, and here ecumenism takes on yet another twist. Said a Spanish bishop: "Our Protestant minority counts less than 25,000 adherents, yet they love to make a political issue of it. Not only is there no persecution of Protestants in Spain, but the Protestants are provocative. We cannot permit sects to come in and proselytize among our faithful. There is much misrepresentation of the situation. Individual Protestants in Spain enjoy exactly the same rights as every other citizen. Only corporatively, as specifically Protestant groups, are they deprived of privileges. However, this too will be changed and full privileges will be granted to their organizations as well." "But," said another bishop, "it appears that the Protestants have been encouraged to intensify their propaganda ever since the Council began . . . We want them to stop this.

We intend to hold a dialogue with them, provided it is done with dignity and prudence so as not to confuse our own people."

As if this were not enough to complicate the picture, we were told by a Melchite bishop that "ecumenism in our country is very much alive, and among all denominations. We have had a certain degree of *communicatio in sacris*. We would not dare refuse to give communion or confirmation to the Orthodox. At the funeral of Pope John in our cathedral, the final absolution was given by the Orthodox bishop of the area. . . ." And from ancient Asia comes yet a final surprise: "In China," said a Chinese bishop, "we have organized the Amity Interfaith Organization to foster and maintain good relations among the various religious groups. We have been working at this for the last twenty years, yet here they seem to realize this only today. It underscores the importance of China and her wisdom, which has often futilely anticipated the developments of things to come." And the same was said by an Indochinese bishop: "We have been practicing the ecumenical dialogue for a long time. This is part of the difference between the Eastern and Western world." And he went on to point out how the central Oriental concept of family, so basic to Eastern societies, would have helped far more to make Christianity desirable and practicable to the Eastern mind.

It was a comforting discovery to learn that in nearly all countries and in many dioceses there have been established organizations and movements to foster the ecumenical spirit and dialogue. Where such initiative was not yet a reality, it was being specifically planned by the bishops interviewed. In spite of being aware of the problems and complexities that the ecumenical dialogue entailed, there was nearly universal readiness to act and to do something about it immediately.

VII

Of Processes and Methods

In the course of the interviews there was a moment of sheer satisfaction: the realization of the quasi-total consensus of the bishops when asked what they thought about the procedure followed in the Conciliar Hall. With the exception of two professedly conservative bishops, a Spaniard and a Brazilian, each and every respondent answered that 1) he was dissatisfied with the system followed in the hall; 2) he desired and expected some modifications; 3) he acknowledged that he did not know how to go about making these modifications; or, if he was sufficiently courageous, he advanced some suggestions.

There are no words to emphasize the striking impression resulting from this complete consensus. It was felt that the whole problem was overripe and badly in need of some drastic solution.

The verdict concerning the system followed at the general sessions encompassed a range from "hardly satisfactory" to "impossible," "a sheer waste of time," "a hopeless mess," and even "a heap of stones with no architectonic connection."

It was universally agreed that the conditions of freedom of speech at the Council had been a very heartening proof of the Church's real attitude and respect for each individual's contribution. But this has been possible only at the expense of efficiency, and has resulted in a waste of time and an added sense of frustration. On the other hand certain problems, it was felt, needed time to mature, and to achieve this even repetitions and delays may be functional. Despite this attenuating factor, the consensus of opinions was that a happy compromise could be found, somehow. The respondents felt that while the smaller groups or lower level debates permitted direct interventions by individuals, at the general sessions the persistent conclusion was that some modifications had to be made if the Council were to achieve some practical results and to maintain interest.

The suggestions advanced were very definite and clearcut. With reference to the whole time-table of meetings, it was strongly suggested that the number of general sessions should be limited to one or, at most, two per week. The remaining days should be spent in group sessions, either by commissions, national conferences or by schemata. There was an almost complete consensus on this: namely, that the discussion should take place in two stages or at two levels.

The first debate it was felt should be at the level of a smaller group, large enough to insure sufficient participation in spite of unavoidable absenteeism, but also small enough to allow more frequent interventions and participation by all those who felt that they had something to say in the matter under debate. This lower level of debate could be the commissions, open to all interested participants, at regular multi-weekly meetings. Or they could be the various episcopal conferences, or federations of several smaller conferences of a whole geographical region when the subject under discussion calls for such alignment of debating groups. Or, as one bishop suggested, there could be as many groups as there are schemata, each group pursuing the debate till they came to a concise and exhaustive formulation which could then be presented to the general assembly for final debate and voting.

While the smaller groups or lower level debates would permit direct interventions by individuals, at the general sessions only spokesmen for whole groups and for a considerable number of bishops should be allowed to speak: representatives, that is, of the crystallized prevailing opinions, both of majority and minority or neutral groups. Speakers representing exclusively personal opinions should, if at all, be allowed to come in at the end of the debate, after collective spokesmen have been heard. This suggestion, it is anticipated, would permit a substantial economy of time; would give individual bishops more scope for participation and intervention in the debate, and would assure a more rapid covering of ground than has been the case until the present.

Whether these suggestions will be accepted or not, the common consensus is, once again, that there should be some opportunity for "real" debate, whereby a statement voiced in the Hall could be challenged and corrected without delay, and the Fathers given an opportunity to examine the propositions critically. As of now, a bishop who chooses to address the Council on a topic must submit his written address three days prior to his planned intervention. The debate, if any, then consumes an absurd amount of time where a speaker may attempt to correct a point made several days before by another speaker, while yet another bishop has restated the question in completely different ways the same day he is attempting the correction. Merely a glance at the daily press releases reporting the addresses in the hall is sufficient to convince anyone that, as one bishop put it, "there was no debate whatever . . . it was just an endless and monotonous succession of monologues, more or less relevant to the point under discussion." An Australian bishop pointed that, should the opportunity for immediate answer be given, this would eliminate the need for simultaneous translation, because there would be ample opportunity to clarify and explain the most difficult terminology, and statements not clearly heard or understood.

The desire for an opportunity to have a dialogue immediately and directly on the Council floor was so persistent and overwhelming, that it made us think with deep admiration of the extent to which the patience and endurance of the bishops had been tested during the first two sessions. The bishops themselves were astonished that, in spite of all these shortcomings, there had been patient and sustained interest by the Fathers in the meetings.

Many bishops made no secret of their desire to see genuine parliamentary procedures introduced and followed in the Council Hall, including practices such as introducing a motion and having it seconded and passed. Some complained that at times the whole procedure borders on mockery: suggestions made and requests voiced fall flat and dead as if never spoken.

An even more basic problem, despite the method of work pursued, is the lack of selective classification of major and minor issues. "We have become too involved," said an American bishop, "in a multitude of little problems, *de omni re scibili*. This has led to a superfluity of topics and superficial treatment of many important issues. We should identify central and narrower issues." And another bishop: "Minor matters are brought in and overlap with large issues; this leads to repetitions and sermonizing. The commissions, unfortunately, were afraid to decide which were the major and which were the minor issues. However, this has not been a total loss because, by discussing certain issues, the bishops have become gradually aware of implications never before realized, as in the case of the idea of collegiality. Even this weakness in the conciliar organization has resulted in greater achievement than we had anticipated. But now we need to rethink this procedure, lest too lengthy a Council result in disaster. This means that we should have a clearer conception of larger goals."

From a different viewpoint, there were two or three bishops who thought that the Council was moving too fast, as compared for instance with the six months' duration of Vatican I. "We need much patience," said a Belgian bishop, "because frequent repetitions in the hall are also necessary. Some ideas must be repeated, and this appears to be the only way to learn, in certain cases. And, on the other hand, we must leave bishops free." Another added: "Because on some issues we found ourselves to have reached an impasse, it is evident that the debate on them had not been long enough, and opinions had not been allowed to mature and crystallize."

Underlying the prolonged discussions and frequent repetitions was the mistaken idea held by some of the Fathers that one needs a certain number of speakers to impress the audience in the hall and to get the votes. Three of the respondents made it clear that some strategy of this sort was followed and that many more speakers than needed were sent up on behalf of a certain issue so as to give the Fathers the impression that there were as many in favor as there were against the proposition. Said an Italian bishop: "Even repetitions are useful, especially in view of their impact on the final voting." This strategy backfired badly. The Fathers easily concluded that some speakers were a poor approximation to a filibuster: "they ask to speak, although they know they have nothing to say." "Each time so and so stands up to speak in favor of a position, that side gets 50 less votes," said another bishop.

It has been pointed out that the patience and active participation of the Fathers, notwithstanding all these short-comings of the general sessions, elicited the admiration of everybody. This is a testimony to their genuine love for the Church and the assumption of their responsibility for her development. The respondents were asked to grade the participation, broadly speaking, of the bishops in the hall. The majority evaluated it as very good, good or fair. Only a few were of the opinion that full participation was confined to a small percentage of bishops.

They rather indicated the factors that make for variability of participation. First is the length of the sessions. Attention and interest obviously simmer down after the first hour or two, and especially after the first speakers on a new topic. Hence the rush for the first places in the list of speakers, the first-comers squeezing the late-comers out. When a well-known bishop and speaker was at the microphone there was rapt attention and everybody was at his place. But no sooner did some conservative bishops rise to speak than there was a mass exodus in the direction of the coffee-bar. In spite of this phenomenon being so evident, the last to perceive it were the people involved. An English bishop candidly admitted that "the strongest pressure group at the Council is boredom. I was so bored that I decided it was a waste to talk . . . the conversation at the coffee-bar on the other hand was fascinating. . . . Often the moderators had to make pathetic appeals to reduce the noise made by the Fathers by their persistent going to and from the bar."

As might well be expected, the lack of interest and participation reached more serious dimensions, and in some cases several bishops voted haphazardly. At least three bishops said that at times the bishops sitting next to them asked them which way they should vote. It seems that there was one bishop who consistently voted *juxta modum,* regardless of the issue concerned. It may very well be that after two or three days of listening to a long series of monologues on the same point, some bishops reached a threshold of indifference and passivity whereby they were not in the best frame of mind to give due consideration to the issue.

The psychological play of group dynamics complicates matters. With profound insight a Latin American bishop noted that: "Sometimes what is proposed as a large problem is but an idea held tentatively by a minority. Yet in no time a large majority accepts and embraces it. While in our own dioceses we feel autonomous and self sufficient, here we want to belong to a group, even if that be a group of chiefs. Unless we persist in a great interior effort at clarification, and exercise our freedom so as to pursue the achievement of truth independently and without extraneous influence, we easily become victims of gregarious feelings and one of the mass. Around the chief personalities, parties of sympathizers are formed. Then intermediate chiefs stand out, like public opinion leaders, and lead the crowd. One is tempted to form a compromise solution between the two currents represented by these groups, without realizing that he is renouncing his own autonomy and originality."

An Italian bishop viewed the same phenomenon from a different angle: "After all, what participation can be expected for instance from missionary bishops who have been away from books for so long and who have forgotten their theology? They necessarily conform to the opinions of the leaders, taking into consideration many factors, such as the literature to which they have access, their previous cultural influence and—why not?—even the material benefits received from the countries of some leaders."

Yet another factor conditioning the participation was the language used at the Council. The candid confession of Cardinal Cushing is a well-known fact; he left Rome and went back to Boston because he could not understand what was being said. Several bishops felt similarly, but could not or would not arrive at the same decision. "Only fifty or so bishops listen to everything," said a French bishop. "I know that the French are very attentive because we discuss in detail what was said and by whom." And he went on to say that the Latin enunciation of only a few bishops could be understood by all. Few understood the Italian and Spanish bishops, because they spoke too rapidly, or the Americans because of their phonetics. All agreed that the Germans could be followed more easily than the others.

And finally, a leading member of the Italian episcopate criticized the oratorical style of some addresses. "What we need," he said, "is a syllogistic way of exposing ideas, a logical presentation, not just emotionalism and rhetoric as often happened. The discussion on the collegiality was basically vitiated by the ambiguous meanings in which this concept could be understood. These had never been clearly defined. How can one give an opinion about something that can be interpreted in five different ways?"

The above collection of opinions, impressions and judgments deals with the most important aspect of the Council as an opportunity for group interaction for the development and renewal of the Church. In terms of ground that the Council will cover, and of decisions that will be reached in future sessions, much depends upon the various factors illustrated above and their disposition. Their right programming may well mean the difference between a very successful and useful Council and the possibility of an anticlimax and a frustrating conclusion.

VIII

Quae Utilitas?

The Gains from the Council

Was the Council worth all the trouble and effort put into
it? Did the bishops believe that some gains had been derived
from the two sessions, and if so, what were they? From the
answers to these questions one felt that he had uncovered the
core of yet another vital aspect of the Council.

The replies were so definite and the consensus so large
that there could be no mistake that such was the actual
situation. Only five bishops expressed themselves in a negative position. An Indian bishop complained that the missions had received very little consideration and had been
relegated to a second place at the Council, as a work of
supererogation. An American bishop regretted the fact that
liturgy was discussed first, because he considered it to be a
peripheral issue. A Spanish bishop remarked that the new
expressions of theology heard at the Council were superficial, and did not answer the need for a novel and original
presentation of traditional truths. A Yugoslavian bishop
said that he was badly disappointed because he had expected
more from the Council, and did not like the propaganda
and lobbying done by the *periti* to get the bishops' votes in
favor of their pet schemes. Finally, a professedly conserva-

107

tive Brazilian bishop said that he disliked many of the ideas
ventilated and discussed during the two sessions, such as
the reform of the breviary, the idea of collegiality, the
restoration of the diaconate, especially a married diaconate,
the changes in the attire of the clergy in many countries, and
so forth.

This exhausts the list of negative assessments of gains
from the Council. All the other bishops had something to
say in support of substantial gains derived personally, and
by the Church through them. Thirty-nine bishops indicated
their novel ecclesiological experience as the most precious
fruit of the Council. To them the Council offered the opportunity to see the Church in a new light, and to experience directly, in a tangible and impressive form, some of
the truths in which they had always believed. The universality and variety of the Church, in her bond of unity and in
her attachment to the center, was most frequently mentioned. For the first time the Church became aware of herself, her strengths and weaknesses, her beauty and
"wrinkles," in the visible assembly of her leaders.

"I felt strengthened by the presence and variety of the
living Church."

"The Council made us feel the pulse of the Church."

"I appreciate the opportunity of participating in this examination of conscience of the Church. I often ask myself
how would I have been without the Council. It has been
a spiritual renewal to me."

"The Council has changed me from a pessimistic to an
optimistic frame of mind. Most bishops were pessimistic
when the Council began. We have achieved a great deal
more than we had ever expected."

"We have felt the vibrant life of the Church, even in the
midst of her sufferings and works, the Church *in itinere,* as
the great mystery and *signum* to the world."

A French bishop: "I never expected that a Council would give me such an enriching ecumenical experience. I have changed my whole conception of the Church." Several bishops remarked that, apart from any objective outcome in terms of decrees or other tangible effects, the Council's basic worth and value consists in the very fact that it could take place at all, that it actually had happened. "It is like making a spiritual retreat: the fact itself of making it is its major achievement." What they really meant had a deeper implication: the Council can be conceptualized as a sacramental entity, a *signum,* homogeneous and connatural to the signified object, a powerful indicator that operates what it signifies. The resolution of doctrinal problems should not be understood as something different and alien to the personal contacts and to the coming together of all the bishops of the world. The physical coming-together is the first step and part of the effort towards theoretical clarification of verities, and the finding of new guidance for the future history of the Church.

It is the fundamental proposition of this study that even the normative and ideological outcome of the Council is conditioned and determined by the patterns of personal and social interactions, and by the group relations that have taken place at the Council. This perspective does away with the dichotomy or polychotomy at times, abstractly predicated of the Church as *"Ecclesia Docens," "Ecclesia discens," "Ecclesia orans," "Ecclesia patiens."* It is evident that we are dealing with one and the same factual reality manifesting in each and every one of her activities the same wholesome and total life. Whenever a particular aspect of the Church is overstressed there inevitably results a loss of balance, and the Church is misrepresented. Such would be the very common temptation to see the Church in her peculiar organizational perspective, for instance, that is juridicism or legalism. Said a Latin American bishop: "I have a juridical mind and feel that Canon Law has a proper perspective from our Western point of view, where the concept of power, or superiority and inferiority, is essential to the notion of right (=*jus*). But *jus* has no place for love. The more empirical approach of the Anglo-Saxons has brought a new element into the Church. Juridicism was stressed too much in the last century, and now a reaction to it is building up in the Church. The Council helped to correct my viewpoint and made me see the Church as a system of charity and love rather than as an external, juridical organization."

This conception explains how a Church which claims to be the repository of eternal, immutable truths, can feel herself to be the *"Ecclesia Quaerens."* "At the insistence of our own leaders," said a U.S. bishop, "we have attempted to bring into the open the major sources of dissatisfaction in the Church, to judge and change them. This represents a startling change, an irreversible process. I am an optimist and I will not go back on this thinking."

As a reflection of the collegiality idea, those bishops who accepted it felt that their understanding of the episcopate had changed basically. "I have gained a new concept of my role as pastor. Now I understand what a bishop is: an inner need to serve the Church, in the consciousness of my union with all the bishops of the World." "I have changed my conception of the function of a bishop," said a Spanish prelate; "I used to think that a bishop is responsible first for his flock and then he is connected with the universal Church. Now I understand that the responsibility for the universal Church is expressed first in my episcopate, and then this responsibility is applied to my diocese as part of the larger responsibility for the Church." "I consider it the greatest favor, the grace to work together with all the bish-

ops for the service of the total church. This has given me
the greatest reward." "The awakening of the conscience of
all bishops for the responsibility they have in the universal
Church, in contrast with the previous concept of a singlehanded chief in an exclusive territory, seems to me to be
our major gain." "The Council has brought about a profound change in me. I realize the bishops' responsibility
for the whole world, as a function deriving from his consecration. This stimulated my thinking, and I experienced a
great involvement in theology."

Yet another major area of gain—this time the beneficiary
being the Church as a whole, together with the individual
bishops—was the increase in the information and knowledge which the Church has gained about herself, in all her
variety and differentiations. A very influential Brazilian
bishop acknowledged that "we had wrong ideas of each
other, to begin with. This was very evident especially during
the first days of the Council. The contacts here gave us a
continental experience of the episcopates." "The first fruit
of the *aggiornamento*," added a Colombian bishop, "has
been to know the needs of the Church today. Before, there
was no such knowledge. A Council was a must. And now
we see it. The real difficulty was to know the Church as she
really is." "Now," said an Italian bishop, "the Pope knows
what the Church thinks and how she feels. Before he did
not know. The nuncios and other information agencies see
what they want, and relate only part of what they have seen.
Now we know the needs and problems of all the countries."
This informative function took place primarily at the personal level. "The Council has given us the opportunity to
know each other and to understand each other's problems,
thus widening our horizons. Formerly we were too inclined
to work in isolation."

"The major gain from the Council is the knowledge that

the center has acquired of the ferment at the periphery of the Church, a direct and immediate knowledge, not mediated through reports of nuncios. This will be very helpful to the 'regimen' of the Church. Disciplinarily we stand to gain even from the tension-release that comes from getting these things out of our system: thus the periphery has come closer to the center. Therefore I would anticipate that there will be very few reforms, if any." The respondent was an Italian bishop and he viewed the process from a typical Curial viewpoint. Even so he agreed that the Council had corrected a major deficiency in the internal system of information in the Church.

Even more astonishing is the remark by a Spanish bishop with inside knowledge of the center: "The Council would be justified if only by the task it has accomplished to make us feel the pulse of the Church. For the last one hundred years the magisterium has engaged exclusively in a monologue. The emergence of so many new phenomena ever since the last Council has caused a tremendous confusion [una baraonda numero uno]. The popes attempted to resolve these problems but to no avail. The Holy See had the information, but it did not help. Discussion too was absent from the Church."

One of the effects of the increased flow of information was a better understanding of the legitimacy of the variety of expressions in the Church. Said an Irish bishop, "We have all changed a little, more than we realize, and this is due to contacts of minds between bishops of different backgrounds influencing each other. We thus learned that the Church has to cater to different situations in different countries." "The nationality dimensions have shrunk," added a bishop from Yugoslavia. "All needs and situations of the Church are represented here from all over the world, in the persons of their bishops. Only now we know the total situation. Even our statements are somewhat elastic, so that they may apply to different countries."

A Spanish bishop, noting that formerly the bishop had a good knowledge of unrelated local problems, concluded that the Church is moving toward "Catholic Pluralism," the understanding of the fundamental harmony between diversity, catholicity and unity. To several bishops this Council represented the concretization of the concept of catholicity, for the first time and in its true significance. In the contacts, communication, and exchange of points of view and information, the bishops have sensed the living church, her unity, universality, and her vitality towards renewal. A U.S. bishop concluded: "A council at periodical intervals would be highly beneficial and desirable. Through close contacts among bishops, the limited experience of an individual becomes the experience of the whole Church, while at the same time the individual's experience is modified too."

By far the majority of bishops spoke of their own personal experience as the chief gain from the Council. When they were being interviewed, the voting on the liturgical schema was coming to an end, and it appeared that this would represent the first finalized decree to come out of the Council. Anticipating this event, several bishops insisted that this schema alone was by itself a great achievement. "Even the concession of vernacular in the liturgy could alone justify the Council as a great event," said a missionary bishop. "We have been struggling for this for many years. It is more than we thought could ever be accomplished." In a deeper analysis, an Australian bishop stressed the implications of the liturgical schema. Historically it signifies the readiness of the Church to go back one thousand five hundred years in her own practice and history, to analyze herself and to change. Ecclesiologically, the schema can be an excellent basis for a reelaboration of the treatise on the

Church as the *populus Dei,* with its stress of the social over the juridical and organizational, and because of the impulse it gives to lay participation. It could be said that the schema contains embryonically all the great concepts that have followed the discussion on the liturgy, and that are to be treated in the coming schemata.

It was surprising to hear the comments of some representatives of the Catholic Oriental Churches. They felt that the Council was largely useless for them, because most of the issues for which the Latin Church was now battling had been accepted heritage in the Oriental Churches, and their peaceful possession and practice for the last several centuries. They felt uninterested in such questions as liturgical reform, concelebration, communion under both species, and collegiality. They were vitally interested in only one problem, that is, reunion. In this respect, they felt that the Council had achieved what centuries of efforts had failed to do: namely, effect a total change of mind within the Church, her genuine acceptance of the concept of ecumenism, as a result of a new awareness of the real dimensions of the Church and of close contact with people and problems. "In the past we have been strongly criticized for attempting to bring this about, but now we have finally succeeded in pulling down the barriers," said a Melchite representative.

We might pause now for a brief moment to *identify the processes* by which the illustrated gains have been brought about. One has already been adumbrated in the value of *the Council as an instrument of information.* The primary beneficiaries of this opportunity were the individual bishops themselves who, distinctly, could formulate their own evaluation and judgment as to how things actually obtained in the Church. This, of course, was dependent upon the amount and intensity of personal contacts, and we have seen that not all the bishops had this opportunity. Many more, though having it, did not avail themselves of it. Nearly half of our respondents were consciously aware that the opportunity for contacts which the Council afforded was among the greatest gains they had derived from it.

"The schemata do not represent much of a contribution: it is the contacts that constitute the most important gain from this Council," said an American bishop. "We listened to so many different ways of presenting the same problem. The variety of it all has enriched us and given an opportunity to know the difficulties of the Church in the whole world."

A rather conservative prelate, although he would not share the enthusiasm of others for such innovations as vernacular in the liturgy and the collegiality of the bishops, acknowledged that the Council had given him an opportunity to know what other bishops were thinking, a previously unsuspected fact about which he was genuinely thrilled, although he remained faithful to his convictions. For many bishops the contacts with their peers and the exchange of ideas served the function of a much needed support, and furnished a clue to help them summon enough courage to voice their own convictions, now no longer afraid of being singled out for their peculiarity but instead sustained by many other bishops. "The Council has highlighted the need for more freedom of speech in the Church. So many things that before the Council were only private, individual thoughts, now have become common patrimony. Now we understand each other better. The Council's value is just to have provided a platform from which to launch these ideas." The verbalization of still fluid and even vague thinking by some clearsighted bishops helped the larger mass to see more clearly what they wanted, although they were unable to express it themselves. Said an American bishop: "We were all ready for the ideas ventilated at the

Council. The big difference is that these, from being the ideas of a few leaders amongst us, have become the ideas of the majority of the Council Fathers. I was one of those whose thinking was rather backward. Now I feel very differently. Then, I thought of them as 'those crazy people,' now I think the way they do. This is the work of the Holy Spirit." With simple humility, a Filipino bishop had this to say: "I came to the Council with my own ideas, thinking that they were the very best. Then I listened to what others had to say, especially the missionary bishops. I soon realized that the others had better ideas than I had."

A Latin American bishop was in an even more confidential mood. "Some time back I had to give a press conference. Nervously I dared utter a few advanced ideas about the necessity of the bishops' participation in the government of the Church in view of the universality of the Church, and about the relationship that I see between the universality of the Church and participation in its power. At that time my words sounded scandalous, the Nuncio to my country was very angry, and I was shaking with anxiety. Now, several months later, these things are common talk and excite no more reaction."

Without sensing it, many bishops had gone a long way in their thinking. What had caused this transformation? We have identified as a first factor the contact and interpersonal relations. The second factor, intertwined with the first but of a different nature, consists in the basic activity of the Council as an intense, high-level refresher course in theology for bishops.

"We are relearning everything," said one of them. "On liturgy alone we listened to nearly 500 short lectures. This makes us re-think our theology." "I completed my studies thirty-five years ago," said another. "I needed to be brought up to date." And a missionary bishop: "Although I have been a professor of ecclesiology, I had stopped at the first Vatican Council. I needed an *aggiornamento* of my theology." "It has been yet another university course for us, restudying our theology and bringing ourselves up-to-date."

Even a European bishop, well known for the profundity and modernity of his thought, found the Council valuable. "The greatest gains from the Council are the ideas and the study which we have contributed to it. In spite of the fact that we [the Central-European bishops] are modern in our apostolate, we still need this assistance. Many ideas heard in the Council were helpful to me because they represented a development of known doctrine both in profundity and specificity." And finally two prominent Italian bishops, although conservative in their orientations, felt that "to unearth all that has been written in the last thirty or forty years in matters theological and to study it was a very useful task. This has brought about a clarification of ideas in the minds of many bishops. Many of these concepts were known, but the Council has added lucidity to them." "We completely rethought our theology," concluded a former seminary professor.

Each morning session saw a dozen or more among the best theologians of the Church give a ten minute condensed exposé on critical points of doctrine. This lasted a full four months. In sheer time it adds up to many university courses in theology, and, furthermore, there were no examinations. But apart from this and from a few minor details, the substance of the Council had all the characteristics of an academic degree program. This was indeed the largest theology classroom of history, and its auditors were the best-qualified people ever to participate in such a training seminar.

The third identifiable process to which many Council gains could be traced was *its atmosphere.* In the words of a Polish bishop, "I liked the atmosphere of the Council most.

It gave us a deep knowledge and understanding of the modern world, of the need for *aggiornamento*. The world wants a purer air to breathe. Pope John has given us the lead, he has taken up the hopes and wishes of the whole world. I believe that the Gospel is going to be presented to mankind in a modern way and that mankind is going to accept it." What he meant was expressed by other bishops in a variety of similar expressions, such as dialogue within the Church and with the world, an opening to the world.

A missionary bishop gave a profound analysis of it, linking the trends within the Council Fathers with the wider image of the whole Church. "At the beginning of the Council, one could have identified two clearly different positions. Now there has followed much moderation due to a greater understanding of one another, on both sides. Each has realized that the Byzantine, feudal and baroque style Church of bygone days is a thing of the past. Our problem is to shed elements unsuitable to the times in which we are living. The clerical conception of the Church is one such thing; but it is like an octopus, you cut off a tentacle here and you are grabbed back by another from a different side. From the individualistic, juridical and Old Testament style legal mentality, we are breaking through to a new spirit, with the help of our social consciousness. We are slowly coming to a new conception of the Church, less clerical and more organical."

The current labelling for this new atmosphere is *"Pastoral,"* i.e., the concern for the masses entrusted to the Church. Although the bishops discussed and studied as theologians, their anxieties were those of fathers and shepherds responsible for their flocks. A well-informed bishop estimated that, in contrast to Vatican Council I, hardly 10% of the bishops present at this Council could be called "theologians" in the strict academic sense. "They are more pastorally minded," he said, "and see the present problem from a more human and realistic approach." This development was received as a pleasant and encouraging sign also by the Oriental Churches. A Melchite bishop noted: "We have gained greatly from the realization of unsuspected dimensions of the Church and from contacts with people and problems. We are especially glad to see that the Church is opening up to the problems of ecumenism and of the world. The contact among members of the whole Church has given an impulse towards overcoming juridicism. Juridicism is the worst vice, and unfortunately it has remained the approach of some churchmen. Originally the Church was not a juridical entity, but merely a Church, an Ecclesia. We are returning to that former concept."

By way of conclusion, we must not overlook one more gain from the Council that remained unmentioned by the bishops, but which surely was in their minds: i.e., experience. Because the bishops were actors and participants in this world-wide play, they could hardly be expected to follow consciously their own performance from the viewpoint of an outsider. But each of their actions and words were being stored in the tenacious memory of the Church, and from them precious acquisitions were accruing and operating. The Council Fathers were quick to learn and to put into practice what they had learned. By the end of the Second Session, things were different from what they were on the opening day of the Council, and it can reasonably be anticipated that by the time the Council concludes its work the Church will have progressed considerably in her thinking, in the methods followed, in her organization and even in her structure.

IX

The Changing Church

"Nuclear" Reactions

One is tempted to cast a superficial glance at the Council, to compare it with the situation in the Church four years ago, and to conclude that things are changing rapidly. The statement may not withstand a strict examination. What is changing? And to what extent is it a significant change at all? And what further implications and developments can be expected from these changes, if any? Two-thirds of the bishops interviewed agreed that since the beginning of the Council there have indeed been significant changes in the Church. They spoke of a "great" change, a "big" change, a "considerable" change, of "important" change, of "conversions," of "evolution" in the bishops, of "growth" in the bishops. This was an observation as to what was happening among their peers, and we can trust that it was no mere projection of their own experience. The extent of the change they observed varies; some saw it in nearly all the bishops, others only in some of them, while still others identified particular groups which have changed. Even so, some bishops testified to having witnessed some "total conversions." But on the whole it was a confirmation and a reinforcement of attitudes held before, or a more explicit agreement with the lucidly stated propositions of respected leaders, and the rejection of those they disliked. On the other hand, the opposite phenomenon was equally observable, the rigidification and retrenchment of conservative positions. This was typically a phenomenon of individuals rather than of entire groups. At worst it was a phenomenon of the minority, the *"pertinaces"* as one bishop called these reactionaries. The change of attitudes and ideas among the most responsive bishops was primarily the outcome of increased appreciation for the opinions of other bishops.

"Now we respect each other's viewpoint," said an Irish bishop. "At the beginning of the Council there were no contacts. There were no prejudices either, but each bishop thought only of his own little diocese. Through the dialogue amongst us we became aware of the viewpoints of others. Many of our bishops had never traveled, many had never seen a Negro bishop before. We had lived in isolation. Many changes have taken place since." The respondent was a Filipino bishop. Occasionally a bishop suggested that one of the directions of change was the readiness during this second session to examine critically even statements of respected leaders. This was the outcome of a process of growth, the bishops moving ahead with the Council. Consequently, cooperation in the performance of the common task became paramount, and the initial self-identification as progressive or liberal gave way to a greater and more dynamic cooperation towards the shared goal of clarification.

The picture was not onesided however. There were at least five bishops who said that they had observed no significant change either in the bishops and the leaders in the Council or in the Church structure. A veteran of many struggles in concentration camps, a charming personality and respondent, had the strongest and somewhat frightening indictment of the Council. Said he: "I am a pessimist and I believe that other councils have done much better than the present one. This Council could very well be the final preparation for Communism. We expected the Council to take a stand against Communism. True, some moderation and relaxation is necessary, following Pope John's example. But the Western bishops do not seem interested in the Church of Silence, and we cannot talk about it. When one of our bishops spoke strongly at the Council, his residence back home was mobbed by the Communists in retaliation." He recalled his personal trials and brainwashing under the Communists, and said that that experience had helped him to "understand what was happening at times here at the Council and in the commissions, where beforehand one inevitably knows the outcome, and yet one feels the duty to stand for his position, although the cause sided with will inevitably be lost." This he envisioned as the function of the minority. This blunt comment echoed the bitterness of his disappointment.

Apart from changes that affected individuals, a number of bishops mentioned changes that had affected entire groups. An English bishop frankly noted that "at the beginning of the Council, the French, the Germans and the Dutch gave the idea that *they* were the Council." In the course of time they all took a second look at themselves, especially the French. "I have observed much sobering of the French bishops. Even the Germans, who had been in the forefront in the discussion on collegiality, when the question of juridical power of episcopal conference was raised, made a turnabout and rejected the proposal." But the groups most frequently mentioned were the Italians, the Spaniards and the Americans (U.S.).

A Latin American bishop complained, "When we first met, the Italians were sealed off from us. Now they have opened up a little. And among the U.S. bishops, hardly anybody dared do anything for the ecumenical movement before the Council. Now you have ten times more ecumenical meetings and organizations." From a German bishop's viewpoint the Italians as well as the Spaniards and the Americans were swiftly evolving and changing for the better, with some exceptions, of course. The Italian bishops themselves were willing to acknowledge that some changes had began to happen that were especially due to their contacts with non-Italian bishops, and there were also some in the direction of an increase in the courage to speak and to criticize what was necessary. As for the Spaniards, a Spanish respondent put it this way: "One-third of the Spanish bishops are old in more senses than one. Yet I have observed great changes in many Spanish bishops, and this is due to the fact that Spaniards were open to new ideas and approached problems with sympathetic feelings."

Spurious factors too influenced bishops in the direction of change. One was the fatigue and exhaustion of the bishops' patience. "When the vote on *'de fontibus'* was taken, the decisive factor that made the bishops put an end to it was that they were fed up with it," said an African bishop. And a Latin American: "Even overwork and fatigue have their say. I saw a bishop vote *'placat'* even before explanations were given as to what we were voting for."

Various group psychology factors determined the reaction of the bishops, such as the very wording of a vote, or the distribution of speakers in favor of a particular issue. "Each time a certain American prelate speaks, the progressives gain 100 more votes, just as each intervention of Cardinal Ottaviani produces the opposite effect. People vote for a proposition because Ottaviani opposes it."

It surely comes as no surprise that a good deal of what went on in the Council could be classified, from a psychological or formal point of view, as an emotional or even an irrational response to stimuli. To prove this, one needs but to recollect some of the most heated discussions, well-reported by the press. In the words of a Polish bishop: "At times bishops forgot about principles and thought more of 'political' consequences. They were influenced greatly by the imagined or projected intentions attributed to other bishops. For instance, the diatribe on the schema on our Lady was evidently an emotional explosion." An Italian bishop, with rare intuition, traced the position of both the so-called progressives and the traditionalists to a common emotional and irrational factor. "The two are parallel and opposed. Both answer a need for the fashionable, for a group with whom to stand. Thus fascinated by words, ideas and persons, we surrender our originality and individuality." This was an often heard complaint. Said a German bishop: "The image effect has played havoc. Take for instance the image effect of such people as Ottaviani, Frings, Suenens, Maximos. There is no room for proper identification and affirmation of one's own personality." "The most capable bishops carried the others with them," said a Spanish bishop. "The missionary bishops, being rather weak in theology, followed bishops from Europe, often those of their native country, Belgians with Belgians, Germans with Germans and so on. Cultural factors, language factors, and even economic factors played their part."

In interviewing some Italian bishops one was impressed by their common leitmotiv, expressed in such words as *"equilibrato," "calmo," "logico,"* and *"dispassionato."* Obviously, in their judgment, most of the Italian bishops had been *"equilibrati,"* while some non-Italians had been wanting in this fundamental virtue. It came as a big surprise when a thoughtful Brazilian bishop was heard to say this about the Italians. "A lack of balance has been noted especially in some Italian bishops. This appears to be the result of a conditioning by political institutions. There are two identifiable groups among the Italian bishops: one, of those appointed during the Fascist era, and conditioned by this fact. This group controls the Italian episcopate. And there is a younger group, less vociferous, because under pressure by the first group. This group votes on the progressive lines. Italian bishops have suffered much and would like to be free. They are fearful of being denounced in Rome; the Curia is an instrument of control. If the Curial system is changed, the Italian bishops would be transformed too. My contacts with the Italian bishops have convinced me that they are open-minded and ready to change, but they need a supporting climate for it." Three Indian bishops concurred in this judgment: "Curia means Italians, though this is merely coincidental, born out of historical circumstances." "To many Italians the Curia means a career." "To a large extent, the Church in Italy is responsible for much of the present situation in the whole world. Here the Church is tied up too much with the State."

Not all the comments were negative, however, as witness two bishops, one from India and one from Latin America: "The Italians, Spaniards and Portuguese were aligned during the first session. During the second session, however, the alliance has broken down." "The episcopates that gained most were the Italian, the Spanish, the United States, and the British. Till now these four had been rather closed in their attitudes. We Latin Americans were formerly thought of as a Spanish appendage. Now many bishops have found that we have a personality of our own and have reconciled themselves with us. The Italian bishops in particular are broadening their outlooks. At the beginning of the Council they did not even talk to us. Now they approach us. The Spanish bishops were even more stand-offish. If Latin

American bishops approached a Spanish or a Portuguese bishop, he was rather cold and aloof. We have observed too that there were limited contacts between British and American bishops, as between Canadian and French bishops. This is a very important problem, but I am afraid we will not overcome it even at the third session."

Changes were not confined to mentality, attitudes, and public images but also to roles and structural positions. Many bishops voiced apprehension at the little consideration priests were given in the Council. "Too much importance was given to the bishops," said one of them. With mixed feelings they all felt that this was "a bishops' Council" as Vatican I was the Pope's Council. They hoped that the next council could be the Priests' Council.

Frequently, however, there were remarks concerning the position and role of the cardinals in the Council. Some bishops resented the privilege granted these cardinals of speaking on short notice, without prior reservation, and first at each session. They felt that this preferential treatment detracted from the attention which subsequent speakers could have received, though they were but simple bishops. A Japanese bishop objected that no provision regarding this procedure had been made in the *regolamento*. Opinions were evenly divided as to the effect of the Council on the role of the cardinals in the Church. Some bishops thought that their prestige was too deeply rooted in tradition, and that the Council would not affect it. Others pointed to the brilliant contributions that many cardinals made to the work of the Council, often as leaders of their national group, and as Council Fathers.

Other bishops advanced a suggestion for a reconsideration of the role of cardinals in the Church—particularly of the method by which cardinals are chosen, and also with regard to extending their function to one more universal and pastoral, that is, on the pattern of the patriarchs. Other bishops felt that the cardinals had lost some of their status (especially under the attack by the patriarchs), and because of the anachronistic association with princely ways and, above all, because of their augmented numbers which affected their status position, a possibly unanticipated (or anticipated) consequence of Pope John's appointments.

Marginal Processes and Post-conciliar Problems

Periodically during the Council a highly structured and formal situation occurred when the process of change reached a decisive turning point: the voting. Unlike any political body of legislators, preoccupied with vested interests and commitments that basically call for a compromise-solution, the problems with which the bishops wrestled at the Council referred to ultimate truths, where there is hardly any room for accommodation, compromise or elusive formulation.

A proposition is or is not an accepted, condemned or dogmatically defined truth for the Church. Whenever a clear statement cannot be made, the proposition will be known as a *"questio disputata."* But, in long-standing theological usage, any proposition regarding faith or morals had to carry some label of a sort testifying to its value as currency for truth and for the deposit of relevation: *"theologice certa," "implicite,* or *explicite, definita," "de fide," "de fide catholica."* Theology text-books qualified each and every one of their theses, often in block letters, with one or another of these labels. The participants at the Council brought with them this mental framework, no doubt, and to each proposition subjected to their scrutiny, unconsciously attached one of these labels.

Then came the moment of truth: the voting. Invariably

to their dismay, several bishops saw the majority of the *"Ecclesia docens"* subscribe to ideas and suggestions with which they disagreed or which they considered dangerous, unsafe, or possibly erroneous. Which side was right? And what of their opinions? Did they have to change and submit to the majority decision? These hints of possible psychological reactions by minority bishops serve only as a stimulation to conjecture as to what a fascinating study this would represent, particularly in the context of the Church's belief in her own infallibility. The bishops were asked to say whether in voting they had found themselves at any time with the minority, and if so, what was their reaction to it.

Let us note that, because of the variety of issues which were voted upon, and because of the various modes in which the voting was presented, the terms "majority" and "minority" were relative and did not convey any significance with reference to progressive or conservative attitudes, unless the issues themselves were listed in these two categories and unless a voting pattern was so classified. The phenomenon of deeper interest here is what are the psychological implications of being with or against the total body, in the context of a group, where "being-in" ideologically, that is, thinking in and with the Church, is the crucial and vital criterion of participation and membership. In the particular context of the Council, allowance was made, by its very nature, for a variety of opinions and some potential deviances; but even these temporary tolerations were merely functional and were permitted primarily for the sake of discovering the truth, which was to be ultimately the real object of adherence and accepted belief.

Of the seventy-three respondents, ten had always voted with the majority, while thirty-three others had voted at least once, or more often, with the minority, in whatever context this could be taken. The remaining bishops did not state their position clearly. These statistics are immaterial. What is of greater import to this study is the bishops' subjective reaction to seeing themselves as being classified with the larger or the smaller group when the counting had been completed. This is of particular interest because all voting at the Council was supposedly secret. Some bishops did make a remark about the flimsy "secrecy" measures, because the IBM cards used for voting bore the name of the individual bishop on them. Theoretically it was quite possible for an interested "insider" with access to the IBM machine room to know exactly how each bishop voted. However, apart from such a highly improbable event, the bishops' vote would not have entailed any public responsibility to their diocese, because they were accountable to no one but themselves as regards their preferences. Having excluded, therefore, any possible public reaction, the outcome of the votings could have only psychological repercussions for the individual bishop. Let us see what these reactions were like.

A Latin American said: "I was never in the minority. After the results of some voting were made known, some minority bishops thought that the Church was going to the dogs, that the primacy of the Pope was all but ended, and that we were almost heretics. Although now they don't label us with such terminology, they are still shocked and astonished." Said a Canadian bishop: "I never found myself with the minority. But I asked myself: is it good? Or have I been carried away with the crowd? If I were to find myself with the minority occasionally it would not bother me, but if I should find myself in the minority consistently, I would reconsider my position with regard to *'sentire cum Ecclesia.'* " And he added perspicaciously: "The results of the voting have at times been puzzling. While the speakers on both sides appear to be equally numerous, the number of votes for the two positions is overwhelmingly uneven. Probably . . . those who disagree with the majority feel the need to talk most."

Another bishop commented: "The minority takes it in good stride, but conversions rarely occur. Voting does not change people, only personal contact and dialogue does." A U.S. bishop confirmed this: "The learning process here never operates a complete reversal of thinking, but only a gradual revision of positions." A few bishops from among those who voted with the minority only once claimed that it was by mistake, or because the question to be voted upon was not highly important to them and hence was not given sufficient consideration. Probably they would have voted differently had they been given a second chance. A bishop from Venezuela: "I voted with the minority once; then I saw that the Church thought differently. I am open to change; I like to listen."

Others had voted with the minority more frequently; some on a consistent basis. They all felt that they had followed their own judgment and conscience and had dutifully served the Church, by giving a sincere opinion. Therefore there was no question of disappointment although their mind "remained open and ready to question many things." A Vietnamese bishop confessed that "it takes much courage to say 'I disagree'; but one has to follow his own conscience and judgment." "This is an affirmation of freedom," said a Belgian bishop. The similarity and concurrence of expressions were particularly impressive. "I have faith in the Church"; "Felt I was doing a service to the Church"; "had no hurt feelings." "I accepted the results, although sometimes I was surprised." "I accepted the outcome well-knowing that the real majority was represented by those who aligned themselves with the Pope." "It is slightly difficult to accept the majority decision. It may be a real problem for those who think they are doing God's will when they vote the minority way." Evidently it wasn't such smooth going for all the bishops. An Italian bishop said: "Sometimes I voted *'juxta modum'* [with reservation] but afterwards I changed my mind and voted *'non placet,'* at the next round . . . these are the dialectics of the Council and should be no cause for astonishment." A Filipino bishop found himself in the same predicament: "At first I voted with the minority . . . but then, after several days of listening, I changed my mind completely. Here you learn the virtue of refraining from a domineering attitude in the presentation of your own ideas. The best ideas can come from anywhere." It may be illuminating to quote at length the charming impressions of four more bishops, respectively from Spain, Colombia, and (the last two) from Italy. Their words are masterpieces of insight:

After finding that I had voted with the minority, I began to rethink my position. I was a bit disappointed, but even so I changed some of my ideas. I had even written articles in favor of positions which I have now discarded. This is the outcome of my working on the commissions. I learned how to listen, and that I could not generalize from my own diocese to the entire world, both with regard to pastoral as well as to theoretical issues.

Sometimes I have been defeated . . . I accepted the decision of the Holy Spirit and agreed with the majority. I did so without difficulty because I believe this is what God wants. But others are frightened and shocked. They cry scandal, because the bishops spoke freely and voted the way they did. Like the old man of the story, they expect the Holy Father to set the record straight, at the end, and show them to be in the right.

The bishops in the minority invariably think that they are right. But when the results are out each bishop questions himself. Am I with the Church or against her? Some of

those who today voted against me, on other occasions
voted with me. I feel I have a duty to the Church to be
consistent and faithful to my genuine way of thinking. With
regard to the schema on our Lady, I felt differently from
the majority. Must my opinion be redimensioned? There
will be no schism at this Council, but there is a manifestation of freedom that makes me uneasy. At times the results of the voting reflect the intense lobbying: the Holy
Spirit may have made use of this too for his ends. I go
to the Council Hall with my whole self and keep my own
individuality. Other bishops, I feel, fall victim to conform-
ism, consciously or unconsciously, especially along national
lines. How can you expect a Frenchman to give up the
aspiration to control the Church?

I voted with the minority, because I felt it was my duty
to say what I believed and to clarify important concepts
and words. Collegiality, for instance, has so many meanings, and unless we define it correctly now, it is going to
be a terrible headache to future councils and theologians.
Rather than confuse the issue any further, let us clarify
it right now. I am aware that I am known as the *"bête-
noire"* of the Council, but it does not matter so long as we
serve the Church and help to establish better definitions.

In the consideration of voting as the ultimate embodi-
ment and climactic point of the conciliar sessions, we can
gather from the above statements a glimpse of the complex
play of human, cultural, spiritual and physical factors that
concomitantly resulted in the final product of the Council.
Some bishops voted one way or another by mistake; others,
due to their old age, voted without knowing the issue involved. At the IBM office one particular card showed a remarkable consistency in voting *"placet juxta modum."* The
majority followed the direction in which their personal
beliefs, their training, the speeches heard in the hall, and
the various and sundry considerations led them. Some
looked to the voting as to the decisive moment of a battle:
"We won," "I lost," "We were defeated" were expressions

frequently heard, with a slight smile and a hint of good humor, after the voting. By means of a succession of polls, the outcome was the formation of a strong majority and the steady diminution of the *"non placet."* The opinions of the bishops were gradually crystallizing in one direction and a consensus was being achieved, which was a far cry from the very divergent positions of the first days of the Council. This process all but confirmed the Church's consciousness that she possesses the truth and that the process of debate and disagreement serves only to highlight the effort which the Church undergoes in her attempt to become consciously aware of what she is and what she stands for. This is a unique phenomenon that finds no parallel in any other congress of human legislators.

X

The Council's Other Dimensions: Space and Time

Because of the central and leading positions of the bishops, apart from the very nature of the Council it was to be expected that world-wide repercussions of this event would be profound. Periodically, the world press reported to the various publics about the Council; in turn, it gave only passing and superficial hints as to how the Council was followed and appreciated in the various countries. The task of arousing interest in the Council during the sessions fell mostly upon the press, both denominational and otherwise, and upon the local clergy. But several bishops realized that, as primary actors at the Council, it was chiefly their obligation to arouse the interest of their flock and to sustain its growth. Those bishops who were concerned with the goals of the Council, and who felt more closely identified with the Church's effort at renewal, worked with outstanding perspicacity and enthusiasm to involve their flock in the work that was going on in Rome. The bishops were asked to sketch the reactions to the Council in their dioceses and in their countries in general; to outline the work of popularizing the Council personally accomplished during the interval between the first and second sessions; to indicate whether any consultation had taken place between himself and his people, and what requests, suggestions or *"desiderata"* were made known to him from his flock. The following statements are the bishops' own impressions of the reactions to the Council in their dioceses.

Almost all the respondents stated that in their dioceses, and possibly in their countries as well, there was great enthusiasm and profound interest in the Council. An American bishop qualified it as "passionate interest." A less-than-enthusiastic response was reported by three bishops from Italy, one from England, one from Australia, two from India, one from Central America, one from Hungary, and one from Rhodesia. All the others were unanimous: the Council has elicited the greatest religious ferment of the century, both among Catholics and non-Catholics. Where enthusiasm is found to be lacking, the reasons given are: either the people are more interested in politics (as in Rhodesia and in Italy), or some Catholics are fearful of the outcome of the Council. "Some of our faithful are frightened about the prospect of drastic changes; they don't want the Council to alter the 'status quo' and they are not standing on tip-toe awaiting the Council's decrees . . ."

An English bishop commented: "Some English Catholics were alarmed at the prospect of having Mass in the vernacular. This was a common reaction with Catholics of Irish descent. Those who had read Dr. Rock's book on birth control were interested in this topic—more so than in liturgy and in the nature of the Church—and hoped that the Council would do something about this matter." Minority reaction could be expected to be conditioned by the local situation, therefore rendering impossible the formulation of a uniform reaction pattern. Even in the same small country, such as Ireland, reactions were mixed, and varied with different strata. Some people, once again, did not like the changes in the liturgy, especially with regard to the introduction of the vernacular. And in general, many of the problems raised for discussion at the Council were somewhat alien to the Irish variety of Catholicism, where one could hardly detect those signs of mass paganism and defections which are observable in other countries. Consequently, the headlines about the Council in the newspapers have often shocked and confused the Irish Catholics. Where the situation was not that favorable, the Council was seen with far more involvement and enthusiasm, although once again for various reasons in different regions. Said a Melchite bishop: "All we expect from the Council is some progress towards reunion. The rest is of no immediate consequence to us."

The bishops probably did an even more arduous job during the interval between sessions than while the sessions were taking place. We found that the majority of them had delivered an astonishing number of lectures, conferences, radio and TV broadcasts; nearly all had written one or more pastoral letters on the Council, and several had organized "ad hoc" activities to communicate with their flocks about the Council. There were also at least seven bishops who, before the first or the second session, conducted a systematic inquiry among their clergy and laity concerning the Council. In some cases, this inquiry was rather extensive, running into thousands of questionnaires distributed and collected. One bishop in particular went to the trouble of asking his people to collaborate with him in writing a joint pastoral letter—compiled by bishop and people, that is—on the most crucial problem in the diocese: family life. The proposal received the most enthusiastic response and the finished product, a profound and modern presentation of family life, was published in a book of 120 pages. It sold 350,000 copies in its original language, and 40,000 in the French translation. A second edition is on the way. Never before had there been such a wide mutual consultation between a bishop and his diocese. Other bishops conceived the idea of miniature replicas of the Council's activity. They invited prominent laymen of their diocese, together with priests and religious, to one or more days of public discussion and ventilation of the problems of their diocese, and requested suggestions to be presented at the Council. These consultations, too, appear to have been particularly fruitful, and have gained the interest of active laymen especially.

Besides these formal consultations, there took place informal and unstructured ones. The bishops were asked to state what requests they had received from their people as specific expectations from the Council. But before giving a summary of these requests, it must be pointed out that, for some reason, the consultation seems to have been more intense between bishops and lay people than between bishops and clergy. Several bishops noted that they had received more answers from laymen. The priests, in several cases, preferred to remain silent, or did not have anything in particular to expect from the Council. There is a deep significance in this fact, and the observation is confirmed by the analysis of the requests received by the bishops. By far the most frequent request was that the Council consider the reform of the liturgy and the introduction of the vernacular, extensively in the sacraments, and also in the recitation of the breviary. This request was made to twenty-two of the respondents. Fifteen more requests, second in order of size, were made to the effect that the Council consider the role and responsibility of the layman in the Church, thus giving him a larger share of responsibility in pastoral and apostolic work, building a system of better relations between the clergy and the laity, and also formulating a theology of the laity.

Other requests, mentioned once or twice in the interviews,

were also made by laymen: for instance, that the Church should intensify her contact with the social milieu; that some regulations regarding marriages be revised; that provisions be made for the formation of public opinion in the Church; that the problem of birth control be reconsidered and, frequently, that the preaching of the priests be improved and made relevant to the times. It is heartening to think that the Council has a realistic approach to problems, and responds to the felt needs of the Church. The reform of the liturgy is the best accomplishment of the Council till now, and the discussion on the role and function of the layman in the Church is scheduled to be one of the first points treated at the third session. This corresponds to the most urgent requests heard by the bishops.

A third set of requests seems to have originated from the clergy, very likely. It calls for better training in seminaries, better collaboration between priests and bishops, a revision of practices and usages with regard to poverty and external aspects of the Church, the extension of the Anglo-Saxon type of priestly garb to other countries, a reconsideration of the attitude towards fallen-away priests and, in one or two cases, also of the celibacy of priests and the restoration of the diaconate.

These are the items mentioned by the bishops as representing the suggestions of the Church members and their expectations from the Council. Most of them have been discussed or are going to be discussed. The schemata were prepared prior to the opening of the Council on the basis of a world-wide consultation with the bishops of every nation, the results of which are contained in the official sixteen-volume edition, published by the Vatican Press.

As the Council unfolded, new needs and requests came to the surface, and it was impossible to incorporate them into the Council's agenda. Some degree of discrepancy between the actual issues dealt with at the Council and the expectations and requests voiced by the Church in general is inevitable. Several bishops were concerned about the possibility of disappointment among the faithful, when the Council was over. This may be due either to overexpectation, or wrong anticipation on the part of the faithful of what a Council can and should do, or it may be due to the displacement of the focal interest by the Council should it overlook some crucial problems in our society. In this respect, the Council's position vis-à-vis Communism will present a very difficult problem.

All the bishops from behind the Iron Curtain who were interviewed said with a certain feeling of uneasiness that the only expectations their people had from the Council were that it would help them resolve their most critical problem: namely, their stand vis-à-vis Communism and atheism. This expectation was shared also by the Chinese. Whichever way the Council will act, almost inevitably there will be much disappointment among Catholics under the Communist regime. This is because, as frequently pointed out, the task of the Council is among the most difficult that could be imagined. The Fathers must take into consideration not only the basic beliefs and principles of morality for which christianity stands, but they must also give due regard to the differential applications of these in the context of varied cultures and people, and above all, to the peculiar problems faced by each community in the practice of these principles. The extremes of this differentiation are to be found in the modern industrial and capitalistic societies on one hand, and the up and coming socialistic and communistic countries on the other. Although the Christian message is the same for both, its presentation and its implications would vary considerably in each case.

The problem is even more complicated when one considers that, according to the various stages at which a particular Catholic community may find itself, the needs-disposition changes encompass a range from a quasi-absence of need to the aspiration for total renewal. The case of the Irish people has been illustrated above. Several bishops (one each from Vietnam, Mexico, Italy, Hungary, Australia, Spain, Congo, Rhodesia, South Africa) were unable to recall any request from their flock. Evidently the tempo of socio-religious maturity varies, as also do the needs. No astonishment is felt when the various activities of the Council are seen in a different, often opposing, light by different groups. Said a Spanish bishop: "Our faithful were greatly shocked and puzzled by some of the happenings at the Council. The conciliar decision with regard to the schema on our Lady, for instance, caused great astonishment. I spoke to nearly 4000 people in my diocese, in order to explain the situation and to calm them down." And another Spanish bishop: "Our faithful desire a larger influence on the Church. But we are not prepared for a more intense dialogue between the laity and the hierarchy. We did not consult our people because they would not answer our questions. They are shy and too devoted to the hierarchy to do so . . . the Council is viewed in Spain with much veneration." An Italian bishop said: "Many of our faithful are astonished at the fact that, according to press reports, bishops are said to quarrel and to disagree. It is difficult for them to understand this. . . ." But a French bishop said, "Before the Council, I gathered together all the most active members of the Catholic Action movement and asked for their suggestions. Many other bishops have done so in France. This was a direct way of knowing what the people wanted. We don't work without consultation with our people. . . ."

An Ecuadorian bishop described what appears to be a

very advanced level of communication. In a diocesan meeting, his flock had requested "that our diocese and parishes become real communities, implying integration of regular and diocesan clergy and a revitalization of vicariates and religious zones. At the parish level, we intend to form real communities, to prepare the way for the diocesan community . . . In this meeting, for the first time we have asked questions and listened to replies from our people. We even ventilated the idea of a common administration of material goods, to take away the resentment that would threaten the spiritual community. . . ."

The differential factor is not only a regional phenomenon, but is also correlated to the stratification system. A U.S. bishop said: "I called a meeting in my diocese, in preparation for the Council, where I also invited the heads of all the organizations. In expressing their opinions in the U.S., the laymen answered with many opinions and suggestions, while the clergy had little to say." A similar observation was made by bishops of other countries too, some of them even speaking of initial skepticism among the clergy. A Vietnamese bishop, on the other hand, said that his faithful had a concept of things different from that of Western society. They did not like to discuss anything or to make requests. They merely accepted whatever they were told and did it. Similar remarks were heard from an Italian bishop, one from Central America, and one from Canada, all of whom mentioned an initial stage of skepticism among the clergy which was overcome, finally.

If we now stop awhile to consolidate the meaning of these various indicators, it might not be too bold to conclude that the spirit of the Council is spreading all over the Church and percolating through the capillary system of communication, revitalizing it. A world-wide consultation and exchange of requests like this has never before taken place in the history of the Church. In no previous council had the social context permitted such an opportunity. The implications of the new phenomenon may escape the superficial observer, but they are nonetheless very basic. By providing the bishops, clergy, and faithful with the opportunity of consulting with one another, and indicating to them the necessity to analyze and to clarify for themselves Church problems in preparation for the Council discussion, our generation has witnessed a new realization of the concept of *"Ecclesia"* as the meeting point of the Catholic organization and the social milieu with all its idiosyncratic qualities and involvements.

Although of supernatural origin and remaining essentially Catholic, by adapting herself to the human features of each society and country, the Church prolongs today the mystery of the Incarnation.

The Council Looks Ahead

An exhaustive scientific inquiry of a phenomenon should include a factual analysis of its origin, a description of the processes of its development, and eventually also an anticipation and projection of future trends. Since prediction is the ultimate goal of scientific analysis, it constitutes also the most difficult part of the same. When the variables at work are too numerous, such prediction approximates more and more mere guess-work. "Where do we go from here?" could well be asked of each participant at the Council. Few could answer with complete confidence.

While the Second Session was being held, apparently the general mood of the assembly changed at least three times. At first there was much optimism; then came the reaction and fatigue of the last week of October. The four-day intermission at the beginning of November was providential in giving the bishops a badly-needed respite, in preparation for the heavy work of November. It was followed by a new wave of optimism and élan. By the end of November, however, in the wake of the realization of the impasse resulting from the abortive condition of the schema on ecumenism, from inaction on the famous five points apparently lost somewhere along the way, and from the unanticipated reaction to the schema on mass communications media, there followed a wave of disappointment and discouragement. Many bishops left the Second Session with confused feelings. While they were glad that they had something to present their people in the line of a justification of their work in Rome, their outlook for the future remained rather grim and cloudy.

Because the majority of bishops had seen in the Council an evolutionary movement and a thrust forward in the Church's progress, their opinions were asked as to the future of these trends. Would they continue, or was there any danger of a setback and involution. Only a very few bishops were obviously afraid that a process of involution might set in. This danger was suggested as a possibility under certain conditions. These were: if the bishops slackened in their enthusiasm and hard work; if the problem of religious freedom and of developing countries were not squarely faced; if no mechanism was established to translate the Council into action; if the proposed reform of the Curia did not become an actuality; if the interval between sessions stretched for too long a time; if there were no adequate provisions for public opinion and correct information about the Council; if some imprudence or abuse were to be committed with regard to the liturgical reform or to ecumenism; if the post-conciliar commissions were to show an inability to implement the decisions of the Council; and finally, if the episcopal conferences should take too strong a nationalistic coloring.

Under any circumstances, it was commonly agreed, some set-back had already occurred and would be present in the future as well, because the initial élan had been too strong and had needed some curbing.

Against these cautious and qualified statements, a large number of bishops expressed confidence that the present trend would not lose ground and that no involution or significant set-back would happen. There might be local opposition in some parts of the Church, but on the whole the present positions would be maintained and advanced. The trend on which the Church has set her course is irreversible and cannot be halted because of the involvement and commitment of too many people. There may be some hesitation and temporary obstruction to this movement, but the main trend will continue. The bishops who take part in the Council have a life expectation of twenty to twenty-five more years. They are committed to put into practice the resolutions of the Council because of the experience they have undergone during the two sessions. Through it, forces have been released at the Council that cannot be ignored. Besides, the bishops will make provision that some guarantee be given for the continuity of change in the Church through the organization of a body similar to the senate of a nation, to assist the Holy Father as source of information and of deliberation in the government of the Church. The best guarantee, of course, rests in the interest awakened among the faithful and society in general. This calls for continuity in the present trend.

One bishop who had done much thinking about this specific idea, and was himself curious to know what form the future trends would take, felt that the Council, as a global phenomenon, was still in its first act and that the principal actors had not as yet come into the limelight. He anticipated significant developments. On the other hand,

he felt that should the "big guns" (the five or six most outstanding personalities of the Council) suddenly disappear,
there would be such a vacuum that the Council would fall
flat. Some of the more conservative bishops also expected
a development of the Council "for the better." They described it as a return to normality, and as the avoidance of
the extreme manifestations witnessed during the first two
sessions.

In general, then, we could conclude that the bishops
looked with positive expectations to the future developments
of the Council, although for different reasons, well realizing
the alternative probabilities that may evolve in the coming
years. At the same time, they were aware and anticipated
what the post-conciliar problems might be. The first and
foremost of such problems could be, according to the an-
ticipations of the bishops, the need to interpret the Council
to the masses in general so as to stimulate in them the same
experience and eventual change that took place in the
bishops. Among the agencies that could "translate the
Council into practice" some bishops mentioned the proposed
Senate of the Church and reform of Canon Law. But the
primary responsibility for the implementation of the Council
would rest with the bishops, and at the diocesan level. "In
many dioceses," said a bishop pessimistically, "hardly anything will be done." The need for some organization (or
organizations) to carry out and continue the Council's decisions was suggested by the consideration that the post-
conciliar situation would present more problems than the
Council itself. After having come to grips with the crucial
problems of society today and having aroused the expectations of the masses, a let-down would be even more dangerous than complete silence.

"Mankind has awakened," said a Polish bishop, "and we
will not be allowed to go to sleep after the Council." Said

a bishop from South East Asia: "The Council has made us realize that we need more meetings to facilitate the exchange of ideas, and that we must communicate and listen more frequently."

"Public opinion," noted an Italian bishop, "has conditioned people to expect fantastic achievements and changes. When they do not see anything striking or of significant fruit from the Council, they may lose confidence in the Church. However, we are concerned also with the long-range effects. The question is: What will be the repercussions of our present decision in, say, fifty years time?"

Two French bishops concurred in the idea that much of the implementation of the Council will depend upon the degree of involvement of the diocesan clergy and the training of priests into the conciliar spirit. A missionary bishop, on the other hand, suggested that the Council would bear better results if the interest of the laity were more activated and if clericalism could be kept within bounds. As in any of the previous situations, opinions were different and markedly divergent at times. The following quotation from a missionary bishop seems to touch upon the central aspect of the post-conciliar problems more profoundly: "What is still wanting is a change in fundamental attitudes. However, the process of change that has already set in seems to be irreversible . . . Till now we have lived a hand-to-mouth existence. This haphazard way will not take us anywhere. The Protestants are better organized than we, with more efficient and effective plans. Among us there is much waste of personnel. We need some change in our organization, by the planning and use of rational methods. . . ."

XI

Communication in Reverse

The Gift of Tongues

The bishops at the Council were not only originators and sources of communication. They were also the objects and receivers of impressions from the outside and, most frequently, the recipients of feedback, since their own actions and sayings bounded back to them by means of the reports, interpretations and comments by the scores of journalists from all over the world who covered the Council in all its details. Further, this variant aspect of the communication system was conditioned by the availability of the basic instrument of communication; that is, the knowledge of languages. In an effort to survey this important aspect of communication in the Council, the respondents were asked to give the number of languages they knew, as well as their reading preferences with respect to international journalistic coverage of the Council.

On the average, each of the respondents spoke at least two languages, apart from his mother tongue, and one bishop in three spoke three languages. Averages are inadequate descriptions of the phenomenon in this context, but for lack of a better measurement it may be well worth giving a breakdown of some interesting details. On a cross-national comparison, it was found the average Latin American, African, Spanish, German, and Asian bishop could handle at least two languages, and in most cases three. On the other hand, the average U.S., British, Canadian, and Australian bishop was normally limited to a knowledge of his native language, while the average Italian and French bishop could usually speak one foreign language and occasionally two. Here is the spread of the average number of languages known, for whatever limited value this may have.

Table V: Rank Order of Average Number of Languages Known by Selected Groups of Bishops

GROUP OF BISHOPS	NO. OF FOREIGN LANGUAGES KNOWN (AVERAGE)
British.................	0.5
U. S....................	0.8
Canadian...............	1.0
Australian..............	1.0
French.................	1.3
Italian.................	1.5
Asian..................	1.7
African................	3.0
South American.........	3.0
German................	3.3
Yugoslav...............	3.5
Spanish................	3.6
Belgian................	4.0
Polish.................	4.0
Portuguese.............	4.0
Central American........	5.0

The distribution is fascinating, but to be understood in its full meaning it should be compared with the breakdown of languages most frequently known. Only this will explain how the French, Italian, German, and American bishops

were at the receiving end of the popularity and were contacted most frequently, both officially and unofficially, by
the bishops of missionary and of developing countries, while
the interest in the opposite direction was not at all of the
same intensity.

The foreign languages most frequently known by the
respondents were, in order of rank:

French	spoken by	45 bishops
Italian	spoken by	37 bishops
English	spoken by	24 bishops
Spanish	spoken by	16 bishops
German	spoken by	14 bishops
Portuguese	spoken by	7 bishops
Dutch	spoken by	3 bishops

Apart from these, several less common languages were
known by these bishops and were mentioned but once, such
as, Urdu, Hindi, Indochinese, Malagasy, Polish, and Croa-
tian. As to the preference of the foreign languages spoken,
some rough indications of the most frequent occurrences
were as follows: The Italian bishops knew mostly French,
and the French knew Italian in turn. The Spanish bishops
were more familiar with French and Italian. The Latin
American bishops showed a marked preference for French,
Italian and English, as did the African bishops. The Asian
bishops were more familiar with English and French, and
less so with Italian and Spanish. German was more popular
with the Latin Americans and with the Centro-European
bishops, although it trailed a long way behind French,
Italian and English.

The respondents, as a totality, knew Latin, of course,
and there was always an avenue open for communication
among them. However, the number of foreign languages
known and spoken by the bishops was highly impressive,

and an indirect symbolic expression of the catholicity of the Church. The effects of the informal communication that formed a large part of the conciliar process were to a large extent due to this linguistic preparation of the Fathers that made possible the extramural interaction, with its far-reaching implications. Inasmuch as this sample is representative of the nationally stratified body of bishops, these statistics are valid cross-nationally within a tolerable margin of error. But because the most representative bishops and communication leaders in each national group were selected for interviewing, it would seem reasonable to regard the above statistics as descriptive of the better educated bishops and to predict that a completely random survey would reveal a per capita knowledge of languages slightly lower than the one above.

Reading Habits

Their knowledge of foreign languages undoubtedly conditioned the reading habits of the bishops while at the Council. These were, however, also affected by many other factors, especially the ready accessibility of certain newspapers or reviews. Some Italian and foreign newspapers took care to distribute, free of charge, copies of their publications to all the bishops present in Rome. The bundles of newspapers were usually delivered to the lobby of the hotels, convents, and boarding houses where the bishops lived, or even mailed to those bishops who lived alone. Apart from news of general interest, the bishops were deeply concerned and interested in reading what comments the papers had to make about the Council in those sessions in which they had been the leading actors. This goes to prove that the bishops were open to feedback information and sensitive to reactions of public opinion expressed through the daily press. When asked which daily or periodical publications they read in order to follow the press coverage of the Council, the bishops made available one of the most telling indicators of Press-Council interaction. Let numbers speak for themselves and relate the story.

This table does not necessarily indicate the obvious: only two-thirds of the respondents knew French, and nearly one-half knew Italian—yet the majority of bishops read Italian and French papers for information about the Council, while in Rome. The main explanation, of course, is the greater availability of these papers, especially the Italian ones, distributed free at times. Another explanation points to the interest of the Italian and French press in the Council. Should it be proved that the press feedback has in any way affected the bishops' thinking, and thus indirectly influenced the Council, we would have to conclude that the part played by the Italian and French press was overwhelming when compared to the part played by the press of other countries. It is not possible to assess the value of this factor on the basis of the foregoing data. The above conclusions point only to its probability, under the stated conditions.

Not all bishops could read extensively, nor were the newspapers and periodical literature the sole source of their information. Many bishops complained that there was little time to read anything apart from the Council's own material, which ran to a sizable quantity. To overcome this difficulty, the most common stratagem was to "listen to others who had the time to read and thus get as good a coverage of the press comments as possible." But the most frequently used device was the various press digests distributed to the bishops by practically every linguistic group. For the German bishops, there was the excellent C.I.C. (Centrum Informationum Concilii); for the Italian bishops,

Table VI: Newspapers & Periodicals Most Frequently Read by the Respondents

Paper	Ital.	Fr.	Eng.	Amer.	Ger.	Span.
FREQUENCY OF RESPONDENTS WHO READ THEM, ACCORDING TO NATIONALITY OF NEWSPAPER						
Avvenire d'Italia......	32					
La Croix.............		25				
Osservatore Romano..	22					
Le Monde............		14				
Information Cat Int...		11				
Messaggero..........	10					
Time Magazine.......				8		
America.............				8		
London Tablet........			7			
Tempo...............	7					
Commonweal.........				6		
Civilta Cattolica......	6					
Herald Tribune.......				5		
Figaro...............		5				
Catholic Herald.......			4			
Temoignage Cne......		4				
Documentation Cath...		4				
London Times........			4			
Quotidiano...........	4					
Daily American.......				3		
Herder Correspond....					3	
Unita................	3					
France Catholique....		2				
Stampa..............	2					
Corriere della Sera....	2					
Newsweek............				1		
New Yorker..........				1		
Daily Mail...........			1			
Stimmen der Zeit.....					1	
Etudes...............		1				
Universe.............			1			
Ecclesia.............						1
Read, in general, best newspapers in this Language.........	3	4	4	3	3	3
TOTAL..........	91	70	21	35	7	4

the *Rassegna della Stampa,* published by the Centro Italiano Documentazione Stampa Conciliare; for the Latin Americans, the CELAM published yet another mimeographed press digest in Spanish. The Spanish bishops had at their disposal four multilingual priests to digest material and to present news in summary form from all available newspapers and from conciliar literature. The NCWC distributed to the American bishops a daily digest of news relating to the Council, averaging three pages, which came out punctually at 6:30 every evening and was "a real service to our bishops," as one of them put it. This was also distributed to the *periti*. One German bishop reported that in his diocese he had a press office which clipped out articles about the Council from nearly 200 papers and sent them to him regularly. Also accessible to all were the valuable press releases from the Press Center and from the various other national centers of documentation on the Council.

It could be said that there was definitely no lack of information facilities, but rather a superabundance and a parallel overlapping of them. With a certain ease the whole organization could be simplified considerably by pooling many of these services and making them accessible to all the Council Fathers. This is advisable because, apart from the service rendered by the Press Center, which was excellent in every respect (though necessarily limited), all other services were structured strictly along linguistic lines, and missed the equally important function of serving as lines of communication to cut across the national boundaries. One detail worth noting is that several bishops read systematically (one of them explicitly said "very carefully") the Italian anti-clerical papers, including such Red classics as the *Unità,* for various reasons. The bishops from Communist dominated countries did it out of sheer necessity for keeping abreast of what was happening in their society. Others had different reasons. Said a U.S. bishop: "Because they reveal facts and give information that argue very intriguing sources."

One can never overemphasize the information potential that lies behind friendly conversations with acquaintances, or that can be derived from an informal open-house for bishops and *periti,* in a relaxed evening. As experience demonstrated, a good listener can get much first-hand news and piece together unrelated bits of information for a realistic appraisal of occurrences, and even for a journalistic sweep of things-to-come.

XII

Who Was Who at the Council

The method of sample selection used in this inquiry was intended to obtain some information as to the leadership patterns at the Council. The procedure used was to ask the respondents to indicate the names of a few (say five or six) bishops whom they considered to be outstanding and representative (and worthy of being selected for the sample), as typical personalities to be interviewed. Apart from mentioning names as requested, the respondents occasionally volunteered only scanty comments about them. If the respondents felt willing to give more names than requested, these were entered too. The assumption of this procedure is that, in the eyes of their fellow bishops, those whose names were mentioned were considered to be leaders at the Council. All told, in answer to this question 283 bishops were mentioned at least once by some bishop of their own or of other countries. Several of these, however, were mentioned more than once. This yielded a numerical evaluation of different degrees of leadership in the opinions of only one bishop, while others were deemed so in the opinions of many of the respondents (at times up to sixteen). The classification used here is relative to this procedure. It serves merely to indicate a basic trend in the leadership array which would undoubtedly obtain in whatever pattern the data were arranged. This offered a difficulty to which there was no solution: the basic statistical data. Each publication about the Council gives a different number of bishops per country and per continent: of bishops eligible to participate at the Council and of bishops actually participating, this last datum depending upon the time when the measurements were made. Fortunately, in this case, the divergence did not lead to a significant error. It is nevertheless highly desirable that more accurate official statistics be made available. The 283 bishops, mentioned at least once as leaders, represent roughly 10% of the bishops listed for all the countries of the world. This is a total larger than the number of bishops actually attending the Council, which was estimated to be in the neighborhood of 2300.

In Table No. VII, there is a panoramic view of the distribution of leaders by continents and some selected countries, and the frequency of their mention by other bishops.

From this table one could construct a summary-theory of the leadership situation in the Church today. The core leadership is represented by roughly 1 to 2% of the bishops. The intermediate leadership bracket may include from two to three times as many bishops, that is, from 3% to 6% of the total number; and finally, the lower bracket leadership extends to as much as 10 to 12% of the Episcopate. Since these percentages hold consistently for the various continents, with slight variations, we can accept them as fairly reliable indicators of the actual distribution of leadership power.

If the figures are seen in percentages relative to the total number of bishops in each country, the difference in the proportion of leadership availability is soon noted. Compare, for instance, the leadership ratio of Belgium or Germany to that of Italy, Spain, Africa or Asia. The reader should bear in mind that one-fourth of the 283 designated

Table VII: Nationwide Distribution of Leaders According to the Bishops' Own Indication

COUNTRY	MENTIONED ONCE OR MORE		MENTIONED AT LEAST 3 TIMES & MORE		MENTIONED AT LEAST 5 TIMES & MORE		TOTAL NO. OF BISHOPS IN COUNTRY*
	No.	% on total No. of Bishops in country	No.	% on total No. of Bishops in country	No.	% on total No. of Bishops in country	No.
Italy........	29		9		6	1.5	386
France......	23		10		6	3.9	154
Germany....	12		6		5	7.7	65
Spain.......	17		3		1	1.3	83
Belgium.....	5		3		3	11.5	26
England....	5		2		2	5.4	37
Austria.....	5		1		1	6.6	15
Holland.....	3		1		1	5.5	18
Others......	9		3		—	—	210
EUROPE.....	108	10.8	38	3.8	25	2.5	994
U. S........	26		10		6		229
Canada.....	11		3		1		122
NORTH AM...	37	10.5	13	3.7	7	2.0	351
Brazil.......	21		3		1		216
Chile.......	7		2		1		31
Paraguay....	3		1		1		10
Mexico.....	3		2		1		71
Others......	38		8		1		273
LATIN AM....	72	12.0	16	2.7	5	0.8	601
AFRICA......	20	7.3	8	2.9	3	1.1	274
India.......	15		5		2		83
ALL ASIA....	42	10.7	9	2.1	3	0.7	417
AUSTRALIA & NEW ZEAL..	4	10.2	2	5.1	—	—	39
WHOLE WORLD....	283	10.5	86	3.2	43	1.6	2676

* The figures in the last column of the table were calculated from the list of bishops to be found in *Elenco dei Padri Conciliari, a cura della Segretaria Generale del Concilio*, MCMLXIII (1963).

leaders were, in their turn, the respondents to this question. As a matter of fact, all the respondents were among the elite of the bishops. The implication of this observation is very important. It tells us about "visibility" as a function of leadership. Because of the concordant (unplanned) agreement among these respondents in indicating members of their group as leaders, about whom they had supposedly enough knowledge to make such a qualification, we would not be far from wrong in inferring that among them there has been a far more intense degree of communication and opportunity for appreciation than might have occurred with respect to other, non-mentioned, members of the episcopate.

Yet another important reflection is suggested by the agreement on the eighteen key figures at the Council. We found that eighteen bishops and cardinals scored more than ten points in this "mention-the-leader" game. Of these, *twelve* were from Europe (mostly from Central-European countries), *three* were from Latin America, and *one* each from North America, Africa, and Asia. The use of this cut-off point arbitrarily, to further identify the few world figures at the Council, brought out the very impressive fact that there appeared to exist a saturation point in the degree of popularity. The highest score was sixteen. The others stayed around an average of thirteen.

In this study of leadership processes at the Council, it would have been possible to inquire further into the leader-ship function of bishops coming from various national groups, as a distinct entity. Because of the invidiousness of this subject, let us only gather together whatever spontaneous comments, or information, the bishops volunteered during their interviews.

Thus an Italian bishop remarked that "Chile is in an advanced position, and the leading episcopate of the Latin American countries." And a Central American bishop added: "The Chilean bishops have the leadership in Latin America. They are very united and well-organized, and have excellent *periti*. They have a national program, came prepared to the Council, and made a tremendous impact . . ." The same bishop said about another group of bishops, this time from Europe: "I have calculated that 73% of the bishops from this group have intervened in the hall at some time or another. This is the highest percentage of any episcopate. However, their talks had neither relevance nor impact. They used textbook theology and talked a great deal."

A Spaniard's comment on the French bishops was that "one group among them monopolizes the action . . . some French bishops are not as free to talk as they would like." One Italian bishop said that "we have no leaders in the Italian episcopate." A missionary bishop commented: "Every conference is somewhat divided, and not one is completely united. The German conference seems to be the strongest and most united in its thinking. I observed too that there was no perceptible link between Latin Europe and Latin America. The problems are different. They constitute new churches and feel a typical reaction to the mother country."

Several bishops noted that the mentality of Eastern Europeans, especially those under the Communist regime, appeared somewhat conservative to Western Europeans; yet they have retained a great feeling of loyalty to the Holy See.

Some bishops pointed to the extensive affinity for one another among the German, French, Belgian, Dutch and some Latin American episcopates. An affinity was also noted among the Italians, the Spanish, and some other episcopates of Latin America.

In the distribution of episcopates, some could be termed

more nuclear, while others would have to be labeled marginal or peripheral. But one group that was impressive for its marginality was the Portuguese. In spite of an explicit search for any clue or indication of communication with this group, there was not one case where the respondents could furnish any information in this regard.

XIII

The Observers Look
at the Council

The communication process received its greatest intensification around the dividing line that formerly separated the Roman Catholic Church from other Christian denominations. The phenomenon goes under the name of "ecumenism," but as of today ecumenism represents nothing more than the manifested willingness to discuss, which represents the outcome of a changed attitude and of more friendly feelings among Christians. The bulk of ecumenical activity has consisted in this exchange of viewpoints in a novel atmosphere. Once again, we find ourselves in the dimensions of communication. For the observers and specially invited guests who were privileged to participate at the Council, the communication flowed prevalently in one direction. They were allowed to be spectators at the Council, and only indirectly and secondarily actors in it. Yet act they did. Their presence and the unofficial and personal contacts between them and the bishops have resulted in the most momentous step towards ecumenism ever since the Council of Florence. Of the many observers, the six selected for interviews appeared to be the most representative. They also represented the largest Christian bodies and inter-denominational organizations. After our interviews, while discussing this last part of the project with the late Father Gustave Weigel, who had been in intimate contact with the observers, he was asked to suggest names of the most representative figures among them. He mentioned five names; all of them had already been interviewed. The reader may regret the necessity for omitting their names in order to safeguard the confidential nature of their statements. On the other hand, it may be of service to the Church to know in general, their reactions to the Council.

After quoting the main questions, their answers will follow almost verbatim as they were recorded in writing during these interviews.

Question I: Did you think of a council for the Roman Catholic Church as possible and desirable at any time before its convocation?

RESPONDENT A: "We never thought of it. It was a surprise to the whole world. We have a tremendous admiration for Pope John for having called it."

RESPONDENT B: "Never thought about it. We have a great sympathy for Pope John, and consider him a charismatic person."

RESPONDENT C: "I never dreamed there could be one. I thought that after Vatican I there was no longer a need for a council, although I was familiar with Catholic liberal thinking about it. We feel much affection for Pope John, in whom we see a charismatic aura not discernible in other churchmen."

RESPONDENT D: "A council such as this was like a dream to me. I believe that Pope John, in his long experience, saw the Church on the brink of ruin while the world was undergoing a rapid evolution. He soon realized that neither he nor the Curia could solve this situation. So he called the

Council as the only way out of the present impasse. In his mind, the Council had to solve the central problem of the relation of the Church to the world. To some extent, Pope John has failed, because the Council became introverted as it were, and concerned itself excessively about its own problems. During the first session, I heard that John complained: 'This is not my Council. When will the bishops understand?' "

Question 2: How would you compare your knowledge of Roman Catholic bishops and theologians before the Council and at the present moment? What are your impressions of the most outstanding among them, and of the various groups of bishops?

RESPONDENT A: "My contacts with them have increased enormously, and I have broadened my views and horizons. I have had personal contacts with Father Küng and with Cardinal Suenens, and Abbot Butler, in particular. As for my impressions about the various national groups, I feel that the Italian, Spanish, Portuguese and Irish bishops are more strict and more conservative, while the missionary bishops are more broadminded, and the Latin American bishops very progressive."

RESPONDENT B: "I have had many intense contacts with Catholic theologians, especially university professors, from Central Europe. Even so my contacts have greatly increased. I have a great appreciation for Fathers Congar, Rahner, Küng, Ratzinger and Chenu, among the *periti*, and for the moderators and the presidents among the prelates. There is a visible dichotomy of two parties at the Council, with the more advanced group holding the majority. It was not so at the beginning of the Council. There has been much significant change since the beginning of the Council, especially among such groups as the Spanish and Latin American bishops, these last answering to the impact from the French and German theologians."

RESPONDENT C: "I knew very few before the Council, and mostly from the area in which I live. Now I have contacted many, especially thanks to the work of the Secretariat. Every Tuesday we invited some *periti* to come and lecture on topics of interest to us, and to answer our questions. This was very helpful. On the other hand, some of the suggestions we made at these meetings found their way to the Council Hall. I could say that I know ten times more bishops and theologians now. The Secretariat has done an excellent job. Now the problem of communication between us is all but over. I feel that I can speak to anyone. Last year, there was some reservation on the part of some bishops; now there isn't any. Before the First Session closed, we had a reception for U.S. bishops. Seventy-five attended. We had another this year, and it was attended by twice as many . . . 'A new day is dawning.' I have a great admiration for Fathers Courtney Murray, Congar and Küng. At the beginning of the Council, I anticipated that the northern European bishops would voice ideas more congenial to my thinking. I thought of Rome as the heart and of northern Europe as the brain of the Church. Now I would not go along with this thinking any more. The U.S. bishops and others are making better interventions every day."

RESPONDENT D: "Before the Council, I knew but four or five bishops and as many theologians. Now I know several hundred of them. My superficial impression is that it is easier to hold a dialogue with Central European, African, Asiatic, and English-speaking bishops than it is with Italian, Spanish, Latin American and Irish bishops."

RESPONDENT E: "I must have known at most ten bishops before the Council, while now I know at least fifty. I noted

that they were very eager to contact me too. My contacts
with the *periti* were especially with Fathers Küng, Congar,
Daniélou, and C. Murray. I have been astonished to note
that the most progressive *periti* were sought after by all.
They have made a great contribution to the Council. Unfortunately, they did not have the direct influence which we
expected them to have. They could not speak in the Hall.
This was a loss because they could have spoken more freely
than the bishops. I missed the laity too, at the Council, with
their capacity to see reality objectively. Bishops are specialists; though they have a good education, theirs is a
peculiar one and they cannot be expected to be open to the
world. I have been greatly impressed by the Latin American
bishops, especially by their concern about poverty in the
Church. They seemed to me to be very courageous and to
have a prophetic spirit."

RESPONDENT F: "Before the Council, I did not know any
bishop or theologian directly, but only through their books
and fame. I met many of them during the Council, although
not as many as I had desired. There is a language barrier,
and furthermore I don't take the initiative in approaching
them, since I don't want to give them the impression that
I am after publicity, or popularity, or that I intend to spread
ideas of my own. I feel like a sensitive flower, that opens
up only under given conditions. There is little time, too.
We have so much documentation to read in so many languages . . . The results of the contacts I had have been
very good. I contacted Fathers Congar, Daniélou, Dumont,
et al., apart from several bishops. My impression of them
is that they are really excellent people, good theologians
and open-minded. Even those among them who are said
to be conservative impress you as excellent, nice and open.
But when the same people act as members of a group or
in an official capacity, they are different persons altogether.

Question 3: Has the Council offered an opportunity for a better dialogue between the observers themselves, as a distinct group?

RESPONDENT B: "I had known some of the observers at ecumenical meetings before."

RESPONDENT C: "We lived together, but we never attempted to identify ourselves as a distinct group."

RESPONDENT D: "Our contacts were facilitated because we had known each other rather well even before the Council, at the World Council of Churches meetings. The Council may actually disturb the pattern of communication amongst us, because of the different concept of communication the RCC has. In our scheme, there is room for everyone and no central point. From a Catholic viewpoint, the communication system is like a wheel, where the Roman Catholic Church is at the hub and the other Churches act like satellites, connected with the center through spoke-like communication lines. This disturbs the pattern of communication between the various Churches." He spoke of a possible "exploitation" of this communication system by the Roman Catholic Church.

RESPONDENT E: "We had no meetings, or common discussion for us alone, as it were, to present a common front. It would have been very difficult for us to do so, because of our varying theological outlooks, and it would have been inappropriate under the circumstances.

Question 4: What are your impressions of the way in which the conciliar sessions were conducted, the system of discussion and the participation of the Fathers?

RESPONDENT A: "The procedure, in general, is good. Although lengthy and repetitious, it gives the bishops a chance to express themselves. But I ask myself: How are we going to do justice to all seventeen schemata? I wish some economy of time could be made. Yet similar assemblies, such as the UNO, also take a long time to decide. I am glad the Pope does not intervene in the discussions."

RESPONDENT B: "I was impressed by the freedom of speech at the Council. I would find it more desirable to have group-spokesmen. I would also like the Pope to participate at the general assemblies, since he too is a bishop. I know Latin and I like to follow directly, but I cannot understand the pronunciation of the American Bishops."

RESPONDENT C: "Some improvements are needed, such as saving time by eliminating the duplication of debates on schemata, in general and in particular. I would like more give-and-take and more parliamentary procedure. Something should also be done to protect the Council against mediocre speeches. I think it is better that the Pope does not attend the sessions; it would have an inhibiting effect on some, or it would motivate others to exhibitionism. The freedom of speech was no surprise to me. The differences of groups, on the other hand, were merely human eventuality, but the reporters exploited the tension to an amazing degree . . . I am surprised we have gotten as far as we did with the Council. I know the difficulties of these meetings because I once held a position comparable to that of Archbishop Felici in my own denomination."

RESPONDENT D: "The sessions are a series of monologues. We have a different concept of what a discussion should be like. Should we be given the microphone, we could not accept the invitation to speak, because we are only observers and not entrusted by our Churches with any other capacity. But in this eventuality, we anticipate that the Roman Catholic Church would feel differently towards us and we would convey a different concept of ecumenism,

quite at variance with the Roman Catholic understanding
of it. Yet we are pleased to note that up until a few years
ago there was an embargo on the ecumenical movement
among Catholics. Then suddenly the dam was broken, and
now here has been a great ferment of ecumenical activity,
but always under the premises of Roman Catholic positions,
which we cannot accept." (He pointed out that the real
clash in the hall actually took place when the *"de regimine
diocesum"* was being discussed. Fearing that the consequences of the collegiality theory would be a curtailing of
their power and autonomy, the bishops came out strongly
against it. . . .)

RESPONDENT E: "Some changes are desired, but we must
also give the bishops an opportunity to speak, or else they
will make no contribution. Some interventions, however,
should be given only in writing. As for the voting, many
bishops voted because they had to do so, not out of an
intellectual conviction. At times, they voted rather *in pro-
test* against something old. It was an instinctive rather than
an emotional voting. Like classroom boys tired of listening
and of being taught, they felt that they had something to
say and that they could finally express what they wanted. I
would expect the present Pope to participate more in the
Council and to be together with all the other bishops. I
regret the distance and the difference between him and the
other bishops."

RESPONDENT F: "There was free discussion, all right, but
it was not democratic. The question as to whether the Pope's
participation at the session is desirable is a very delicate one.
The psychological attitude on the part of non-Catholics is
that, even granted the primacy attribute, the Pope is still a
bishop and part of the Church. We understand the dilemma
and implications of this: the Pope can be in the Council

only by considering himself to be one of the bishops. On the other hand, we appreciate the fact that the Pope, if he is infallible, by his own infallibility has been taught to not use it. This may sound like words, but it carries meaning. We are convinced that in spite of our divisions God rules and acts in history. Although the method of discussion followed at the Council is not practical but rather time-consuming and fatiguing, it is an excellent idea to afford the opportunity of hearing the voice of the entire Church. From our advantageous viewpoint, unknown to you, we are aware of what the Church needs for a renewal: a sense of priorities. It is a common failing of all Christians to cherish a great love for discussion and rhetoric. We easily fall victim to the temptation to take a long-range look at things, starting from Adam and Eve and going all the way to the eschatological coming of Christ. I am a victim of this illness myself. These, however, are styles for journals and for the meetings of specialists, and not for a general council. Here you have the general staff of an army (the Church), and in war you don't discuss the theory of war but rather the methods of achieving victory. If divine providence does not intervene, this Council will last as long as the Tridentine. Too many topics are discussed and too many details are voted upon. While you discuss, someone else acts and carries out his plans."

Question 5: What gains in your opinion have been derived from the Council, and what is your reaction to the ideas you have heard in the Council?

RESPONDENT A: "I saw the eagerness for unity within Christianity, felt with a sense of urgency. If some adjustments were made, it would be meaningless to speak of who joins what or returns to whom. I agree as to the need for a head of Christianity. The more important question is:

What should the Pope's power be? And, who elects the
Pope? The whole world should. Election and power are
the critical factors from our viewpoint."

RESPONDENT B: "The opportunity for contacts constitutes
the chief gain from the Council. We were not surprised at
the ideas heard there. We had anticipated that it would
be difficult to hear them spoken so openly."

RESPONDENT C: "I gained much from my acquaintance
with the theological thought of the Church and with the
Church's life and procedure in general. I liked particularly
attending Mass every day and being able to pray together
with the Roman Catholic Church. I believe that intercon-
fessional prayer meetings would help much in the effort
towards unity. I was surprised and delighted to hear so
many bishops call for the vernacular, and show a deep
interest in Scripture. I felt that the Church is growing and
becoming progressively more liberal. From the hesitation
of the first days, we have come to a 60/70% majority. We
heard even conservatives pay lip service to ecumenism.
Most of all we were surprised to note that the Latin American bishops weren't all the conservatives we had thought
them to be."

RESPONDENT D: "Although new avenues of communication
have been opened between the Roman Catholic Church
and other Churches, we have the impression that these new
channels are exploited in favor of Roman Catholicism rather
than used as a reciprocal line of exchange."

RESPONDENT E: "The greatest gain is the conversion of
many bishops ("conversion" is a strange word to use). It
means that we have come together and seen the Church in
a new light other than the one to which we are accustomed.
Many observers have also been converted to new views.

Aside from this, the decrees of the Council will be parliamentary papers, compromises, with the exception of the liturgical schema."

RESPONDENT F: "Our greatest enrichment is the growing conviction that the Roman Catholic Church is trying to find a way . . . it may be at first an unsuccessful effort, but it has begun and it will continue . . . I liked the changed attitude as regards Latin—the use of a specific language is unimportant today. It is clear to any reasonable person that all nations are equal before God and that all cultures have an equal claim to reproduce the Gospel and to preach the truth. Latin has no better qualification than other language. Latin once had its value as an external instrument of unity in the Church. Now Christianity has been exported from Europe and the situation has been basically changed, through technological progress, the unification of the world, the emergence of historically rival cultures in Asia and Africa, and through the spread of secularism and atheism. The European culture assumes a secondary function, and is no longer the root and center of world culture. With it, Latin has lost its former position. Nothing has impressed us as new in the schemata. What does seem new is the question about the necessity of divine intervention, through some theological genius, who could find a formula to combine the idea of collegiality and the primacy of the pope. At present it is at a deadlock; if someone can find this formula, he will be like a savior. . . "

Question 6: What is the reaction of your Church to the Council, and what future development do you anticipate?

RESPONDENT A: "From indifference to the Roman Catholic Church, we have now moved to a feeling of great expectations, because there has been an increase of communication among us. There is always a danger of reversing the present positions, and we must pray much. Many people pray for reunion. I received a letter from some Polish seminarians assuring me of their prayers, which is very touching. We now realize the impossibility of living in isolation, and how, by coming together, we can solve our problems."

RESPONDENT B: "During the interval between sessions, I reported to the supreme body of my Church. We have great expectations in the Council and faith in God. We would see with appreciation some improvement with regard to religious liberties in Spain and in Latin America, the mixed marriage regulations of the Roman Catholic Church, and more collaboration in practical fields. I feel that the present trend in the Church will not stop; it would be too difficult to do so. I am under the impression that the Council is actually made by a small group. . . ."

RESPONDENT C: "I never talked on anything more popular among my people. With Pope Paul plowing along the same furrow as John, I do not anticipate any reversal of trends. The bishops now know what they believe, and the collegiality idea gives them added strength."

RESPONDENT D: "Certain processes are irreversible. And the present process in the Roman Catholic Church is one of these. I could not identify the forces that would bring the momentum of the Council to a stop. So many expectations and hopes have been built up that it would be disastrous to leave them unfulfilled. Although the Church claims that the current changes are not substantial, but that it is only a question of presenting in a new form what has always been there, I believe that the changes in the Church go deeper than that. Certain modifications in the Church are substantial, but they must not be presented as such because of the theological necessity of claiming continuity, of being identical with oneself, *so as to legitimize the claim to represent the only Church traditionally derived from Christ.* This is a central point. When the Roman Catholic Church will accept the idea that change as such is not to be excluded, but to be accepted without coloring it, then the dialogue will be easier."

RESPONDENT E: "During the interval, I spoke at length about the Council. In my country there is a tremendous interest in it. Now I feel that in my own Church we should begin the same self-criticism and self-analysis in which the Roman Catholic Church is engaged. We feel a strong need to bring our Church up to the same level as that of the Roman Catholic Church. At the beginning of the Council, some of our members were critical and pessimistic and refused to recognize the fact that something very real was happening in Roman Catholicism. I am optimistic: there is no stopping this movement; you can no longer reinstate an authoritarian regime in the Church—the younger generation will not tolerate it. If the Church does not want to die, this movement must continue, or we will have an internal revolution. I hope that there will be more people sufficiently courageous to break through the ecclesiastical boundaries toward prophecy. In the Hall there were some speakers with prophetic spirit, and when they spoke there was silence and enraptured attention. 'Now the Council is moving on,' everybody felt. Now the ice is broken, and the ship made seaworthy. In future relations with the Roman Catholic Church we will be compelled to go deeper, because it is a new Church we are facing, and to work with her will be more useful and fruitful. Every theology from now on will of necessity be ecumenical. We must bring in the *other,* always, and we should try to go together in the world because the separation between the Churches is of far less gravity than the confrontation and separation between the Church and the World. Let us face the World together. . . ."

RESPONDENT F: "My Church appreciates my role here, or else they would not have sent me again for the Second Session. We represent no exception to the world's appreciation of the Council and of Pope John. At his death, we had a special funeral service for him, the first time in centuries we did so for a pope. As for the future, we feel that the Roman Catholic Church is trying to find her way, but has found no solution as yet. How far will she go? We wish and pray. In our relations, there are two aspects to be considered, the psychological and the dogmatic. For the dogmatic aspect we are waiting for the Council's decision. But we have already begun with the psychological factor. There are very good relations at the high levels. But it is not enough until this attitude seeps down into the lower level. This is very important, especially for the impression we make on non-believers."

A common remark made by these observers referred to their appreciation of the work done by the Secretariat for Promoting Christian Unity, led by Cardinal Bea, and the assistance given, including the various parties and invitations, several of which the observers reciprocated. Theirs was a genuine gratitude, and indeed no praises could suffice to describe adequately the excellent work done by this dedicated group of men.

These pages let the observers speak for themselves, and render their words as faithfully as possible. The valuable insight which these last few pages give fully justify the necessity of abundant quotations in this chapter.

XIV

The Last Council?

After the foregoing presentation of opinions and comments by the various respondents in this study, it is perhaps permissible to add a few reflections which have been suggested only indirectly by the data contained in the preceding pages. These observations are presented here as a stimulus to the consideration of possible alternatives and, as such, they are subject to discussion and modification.

The day Pope John announced that another Council was forthcoming, he may, or may not, have realized that in so doing he was setting in motion the most profound change to take place in the history of the Church for the last four centuries. He may not have perceived, either, that his Council would probably be the last of its kind. In its structure and procedure, in the number and variety of its participants and in its meaning, Vatican II can be said to give evidence of being the conclusion of the series of "modern" Councils, that began with the First Lateran Council in the 12th century. Though this may sound like an unsubstantiated anticipation of future events, the reader should not shy away from considering the possibility that future Councils, *as group phenomena,* may have characteristics basically different from the present Council and those that went before it.

Historically, we find that councils have been convoked

periodically, at the request of popes, or emperors, a decision determined by the emergence of crises and problems resulting from changed conditions in the Church and/or in society. Because in the past it took a longer time for crises to emerge and to clamour for a solution, the frequency of Councils has varied. But from the year 325 to 1545 there has been (with the exception of the 9th and 10th century) at least one council in each century, and there has been an average interval of 65 years between Councils. The Council of Trent stood in a class by itself and through an amazing combination of historical events, conscious policies, ideological rigidification and reaction to Protestantism, it effectively did away with the idea of holding a Council at periodical intervals, while mankind was going through the most turbulent centuries of its history and a new world was being molded. Whether this represents a gain or a loss for the Church is subject to discussion.

The first Vatican Council was a seeming exception to the pattern in force after Trent. But, in the process, it actually confirmed the general impression that the Conciliar era had ended. With the definition of Papal infallibility, the Catholic world and many non-catholics moved swiftly to interpret the implications of the Council's decision: this had been a Council to end all Councils. As has already been pointed out, prior to 1958 a majority of the Bishops held the quiet conviction that, after Vatican I there would be no more need for, or meaning in, another Council.

Pope John's sudden inspiration disturbed this mode of thinking and set imaginations afire with the prospect of unsuspected hopes. It opened up the possibility of re-examining positions and attitudes securely held ever since the Council of Trent and it suggested that the reform of the Church was still a task to be accomplished. But, in the centuries that followed Trent, the world had moved rapidly

and widely and it was now felt that the Church was facing
a larger backlog of problems than she could handle in her
ordinary administration. Many respondents in our study,
it will be remembered, complained that the Council was
concerning itself with a multitudinous variety of problems;
yet it could not be otherwise, considering that this was a
work overdue for four centuries and more. Given the rate
of speed at which Vatican II has been moving in its first
two sessions, it seemed to some that the Council could not
hope to do justice to its program in less than the time it
took its predecessor at Trent.

In our industralized society, however, the concept of
time has changed: by the time the present Council, whatever
its duration, is over, new and serious problems may have
arisen, some of them created by the Conciliar "situation"
itself. From the preceding pages it has been clear how pressure is building in favor of changes in the number and
modality of general sessions, the topic discussed, the mode
of interventions and the choice of speakers. In yet other
direction, there is a surging demand for wider participation
in the Council by theologians and laymen, and in general
for a more varied representativeness of the different strata
of the Church. Thus, the pressure of history and social conditions suggests the possibility of re-analysis of the conciliar
system as a mechanism of resolution of crises in the Church.

This is suggested also by the consideration of the number
of participants at the Council. From this viewpoint, the
Council appears to be somewhat unwieldy. Of the 2676
bishops officially listed in the "Elenco dei Padri Conciliari"[1]
(the "Peregrinatio Romana ad Petri Sedem" lists 2857
bishops), only a daily average of 2135 bishops attended the
meetings, according to the statistics given in the daily bul-

1. *Elenco dei Padri Conciliari,* a cura della Segretaria Generale
del Concilio, Roma, Settembre 1963.

letin of the Press Office for the second session. Of these a minority of not more than 10% could be said to have made substantial contributions and exercised some effective leadership, other than listening to speeches and voting. A German peritus bluntly reflected that: "plus aut minus non mutat essentiam . . . Was there a real need—he said— to call 2800 bishops together, when a fraction of them could have done an equally good, if not better, job? The Council is too heavy and the number of participants makes no real difference: furthermore, in spite of their coming together, you don't really know, after a session, what the Fathers actually think. Many bishops need far more explanations about the topics under discussion. When they don't understand, they vote 'placet juxta modum' . . ."

Unknowingly, the several hundred absentee bishops (for whatever reason) contributed to the mitigation of the evil. But this is tantamount to say that nearly one in five bishops was absent from the Council, and their absence made no apparent difference to it.

If we project the present situation to a generation, or two, from now and take into consideration the inevitable natural increase of dioceses and bishops, we may wonder at the thought of an even larger number of bishops which would have to take part in eventual Conciliar sessions. The experience of the last two sessions seems to indicate that due to the large number of participants (and their interventions) and because of the gravity of the problems on hand, the Council operates somewhat clumsily, imposes a heavy strain on the time and money of the hierarchy and, ultimately, favors the enterprising minority in manipulating the majority to its own goals. At the base of the difficulties that beset the Conciliar system, as any other system of human deliberation, there is the crucial problem of change in a large-scale organization. Historically, all would agree that there have been repeatedly vast changes in the Church, not in her "essential" aspects, but, definitely, in their presentation, and in those aspects of her organization and normative system that are bound to and conditioned by a particular time and culture. The main fault with this process of change and necessary adaptation has been its sporadic and almost "traumatic" occurrence, usually delayed and accepted only when the pressure had attained to almost intolerable levels, or, as it happened at Trent, when the dam had already broken and the waters of turmoil had flooded the earth. The question could be asked: *what prevents the Church from facing this problem of change as an ongoing process, systematically solving new problems as they arise, without letting them grow to critical proportions or cumulate, unsolved, until a council is convoked?* We are faced here with an instance of the wider sociological dilemma between administration and innovation, bureaucracy and charisma, the juridic and the organic approach. History is teeming with people and events who, at different times, fell into one or another of these categories.

What appears to be a viable solution in modern society could eventually be extended and applied to the Church as well: this would be the *institutionalization of change itself*: that change, that is, which is deemed necessary, useful, and above all timely in the Church at a given moment and in a given place. Such institutionalization will call first of all for a *theoretical justification of what has, as a matter of fact, taken place in history*—namely, that *the Church has periodically adapted herself to varying situations and social conditions, and that this has proved healthful and useful for the achievement of her goals.* From this the conclusion leads to a realization that the Church has the duty to be continuously vigilant and on the move, lest she find herself so involved in temporary and particular situations that her major objectives are lost sight of. Only a *mechanism of ongoing self-analysis* and a *periodic taking-stock of herself* can assure this over the years.

The assumption behind this hypothesis is that such a mechanism exists, and more important, that a functioning system of communication and examination of what actually is happening can be found, year after year, in the Church. This assumes that there be accurate and reliable information available as a prerequisite to any attempt to evaluate objectively the Church's situation and development around the world. The shortcomings of the system of communication in the Church which held before the present Council has been sufficiently emphasized by the statements of the bishops quoted at the beginning of this book. As a *peritus* very well acquainted with the Roman situation said: "Vatican representatives went to the periphery and brought back to the center what they thought—that is, their own ideas and convictions, not the real image of the situation . . ."

But information alone would not be sufficient, even if accurate. It must be continuously evaluated and analyzed with scientific detachment, bearing in mind the objectives of the Church as the organic community of the followers of Christ. It is evident that any vested interest militates against scientific observation and analysis. Unfortunately, no systematic use has been made, in the Church, of the social scientist, who could prove of invaluable help by placing at the service of the Church the cumulated knowledge of behavioral sciences, by gathering necessary information and, through analysis of available data, contribute to the planning for the Church's future. This does not appear to have taken place for the Church as a whole: whenever it has occurred, it has been a phenomenon of limited proportions and confined to local levels. In the context of a conciliar situation the usefulness of a scientific approach may extend even to the fundamental problems that have been identified here. These problems, from the present study, could be summarized as follows:

1) How *to use and channel* to purposive and fruitful goals *the interaction of Church leaders at the Council, as a valuable resource in itself.*

2) How to establish *a mechanism of ongoing change and adaptation* of the Church to continuously changing social situations, to function as a carry-over of the Council's spirit.

3) How to *keep the channels of communication* within the Church *functional and expanding* with the growth of the organization itself.

Points 2 and 3 indicate the necessity that a functional alternative should be found, apart from the conciliar system, to complete and continue the function that councils perform in the Church.

In the light of the partial reforms and changes which have taken place in the Church since the idea of aggiornamento has been enkindled for us through John XXIII, we realize even more acutely how sad the former state of things was—and this only a few years ago.

But few may have paused to ask the crucial questions: *why and how has this situation come about, and how could it endure until the Council?* And: *what is the guarantee that a similar situation may not emerge again, and how can we prevent this from happening?*

Could then the highly concentrated function of sporadic councils be *spread and decentralized over time and space,* to bring about a gradual and progressive achievement of what normally would be a council's objectives? This question calls for some consideration.

The council's objectives could possibly be achieved through other means, as for instance, through a graded hierarchy of consultations, at the regional, national and continental level, and finally, through a body of world-wide representation. These could be significantly smaller in number than a Council, would be capable of meeting much more frequently, making important decisions and facing new problems as they arise, while having access to information representing factual situations and the variety of the Church's experience throughout the world. In the course of these interviews several bishops came out openly in favor of a "Senate of the Church." During the seventh week of the Second Session "rumors" that an explicit request by a group of bishops for the formations of such a senate would be presented to the Holy Father reached a very high pitch in Rome.

What apparently would be missed in such substitution is the valuable experience made available to the bishops in a council, and which contributed to the revitalization of their faith as leaders of the Catholic community, strengthening the Catholic spirit, and making available to them information and contacts that broaden the bishops' horizons so that they can grasp the real dimensions of the Church throughout the world. However, there appears to be no reason why this experience should not be had, as *a worthwhile objective in itself,* in periodical universal meetings of the episcopate: a stepped-up and intensified celebration of such things as the Holy Year, or the International Eucharistic Congresses, or even the election of a pope.

As for the mutual information function that Vatican II has provided, it must be noted that this was an unanticipated by-product and an unplanned consequence of it. Little, if any, direct provision was made to create those conditions that would have made for maximum interaction among the various groups of bishops, nationally and internationally. Whatever informal system of communication and informative interaction took place at the Council, it arose spontaneously and gradually, at times overcoming oppositions and difficulties from official and unofficial sources, simply because the need was so urgent and the opportunity so great. Everyone is agreed that to accommodate 2200 people for two months in a single place, or within a limited area in a city like Rome, is not an easy project at all. On the other hand, to distribute 2200 bishops with a compulsory three-hour-a-day rendezvous throughout ninety different institutes scattered all over Rome, some of them twenty-five miles apart, after having convoked them from all points of the globe, seems like the ultimate frustration of a most beautiful plan. Yet this was the geographical spread of the bishops' accommodations in Rome. Although willing to meet and know each other, many bishops found it impossible because of the physical distances, the necessity to travel across town (and the Roman traffic can be very disastrous), and the limited time available.

The benefit derived from the *"Concilium"* in terms of personal encounters and informativeness was to a great extent merely accidental and, in fact, the full potentialities of the Council in this respect were never systematically tapped or exploited. The spontaneous solution to this situation was for each bishop to limit his contacts within the manageable range of national groups, and occasionally within continental groups of bishops, as can be seen from the tables. In the particular case of the Italian bishops, as we have seen, because of their very large number and their even wider spread all over Rome, not even the Council afforded an adequate opportunity for them to know each other sufficiently and to achieve a tangible degree of group-homogeneity. On the other hand, to give another instance, the Brazilian bishops (admittedly only 216 strong as compared with the 386 Italian bishops) appeared to have achieved a higher degree of group-homogeneity and consensus, and most of the time acted as a coordinated body when it came to voting or to interventions in the hall. This may be attributed to the availability of capable leadership among them, but also and above all to the fact that the majority of the Brazilian bishops lived together at the Domus Mariae, and were in constant contact with each other. Here at their disposal they had an excellent complex of facilities, including a library, a score of lecturing *periti*—even a local comic newspaper, the *Conciliabulo*—and a number of little things that made their stay there very enjoyable and fruitful. If the Council is understood not only as a dogmatic inquiry but *as an experience,* something similar to the conditions which prevailed at the Domus Mariae is a necessary component. Can a future council handle this problem? Some of the marginally located bishops complained that in spite of the numerous libraries and institutions of ecclesiastical higher learning in Rome, they didn't have even a copy of canon law to consult. And these were not isolated cases.

A French theologian, an adviser to some prominent French bishops, said that in his opinion, the present Council should have been held in a city other than Rome, one where better facilities would be available and—above all—where the atmosphere would be less suggestive of the past four centuries with all their historical connotations. The aim, as he saw it, would be to put the bishops more at ease, and give them courage to face the problem of a modern world. Not seldom in the past councils were held in cities other than Rome, and they, too, were fruitful.

The gist of this argument is to call attention to the large component of a council: that is, its informal structure and network of relationships. The Council Fathers are human beings, and the future of the Church depends upon the action and interaction of their personalities. The best results can be expected only when they gather in a manageable number, and under such conditions that their gathering together is a complete and symbolic expression of the Church's vital capacity for self-regeneration and perfection. Here again the contribution of the social scientist might have proved particularly valuable.

The parable of the Gospel tells us of the man who, wishing to build a tower, felt the obvious need to sit down and quietly figure out the expense involved, and to sketch the blueprints of his project. In the modern development of things, there may be useful room for those who can help plan and carry out the continuous building of the tower of God that is the living Church.

Index

Absenteeism, from council, 178; from episcopal conferences, 56

Acquaintances, made during Council, 80-86

Africa, 49, 56, 60, 61, 96, 156, 157, 158, 171; bishops from, 29, 68, 69, 75, 76, 79, 80, 81, 82, 85, 86, 88, 91, 123, 140, 148, 149, 164, 171

Aggiornamento, 26, 27, 30, 32, 33, 38, 43, 45, 111, 117, 118

America, magazine, 152

American Press Panel, 65

Americana Hotel, 72

Americanism, fear of, 65

Amity, Interfaith Organization, 98

Anglo-Saxons, 110, 138

Annuario Pontificio, 49, 50

Arab countries, 60

Argentina, 50, 80, 81; bishops from, 71, 74, 75, 140

Asia, 49, 60, 61, 68, 81, 82, 88, 96, 156, 157, 158, 171; bishops from, 69, 82, 86, 90, 91, 148, 149, 164

Australia, 50, 60, 69, 72, 80, 81, 82, 83, 96, 135, 140, 157; bishops from, 35, 102, 113, 148

Austria, 81, 82, 83, 157; bishops from, 50, 76

Avvenire d'Italia, 152

Baltimore, Third Plenary Council of, 63

Bea, A., Cardinal, 174

Belgium, 49, 69, 81, 87; bishops from, 82, 83, 86, 93, 103, 124, 139, 148, 156, 157, 159

Bildarraz, F., 51

Birth control, 138

Bolivia, 50; bishops from, 72, 76, 80

Boston, 105

Brazil, 50, 60, 72, 76, 80, 81, 82, 157; bishops from, 72, 73, 74, 76, 85, 99, 108, 111, 183, 184

Butler, C., Abbot, 163

Caesar Augustus Hotel, 71

Camara, P. Helder, Archbishop, 72

Cameroon, 49, 72

Canada, 50, 60, 61, 69, 72, 77, 80, 81, 82, 83, 86, 87, 157; bishops from, 38, 43, 69, 84, 85, 126, 141, 148

Canon Law, revision of, 78, 110, 145

Catholic Action, in Italy, 59

Catholic Herald, newspaper, 152

C.E.I., (Conferenza Episcopale Italiana), 57-62, 89

CELAM, 68, 72, 73, 153

Central America, bishops from, 29, 51, 82, 135, 141, 148, 158

Centralization, in episcopal conferences, 54

Change, in the Church, 18-20, 179-80; in communication process, 18-19; desired by bishops, 72, 75, 158-159; dynamics of, 123-25; of groups in the council, 122-26; institutionalization of, 179; as seen by observers, 172; of structures, 20

Chenu, M. D., 163

Chile, 50, 72, 80, 157; bishops from, 72, 75, 158-59

Mexico, 50, 60, 81, 82, 157;
bishops from, 72, 74, 75, 140
Minority, effect on bishops, 128-133
Missions, bishops from, 32, 37, 40, 41, 42, 81, 88, 146
Monde, Le, newspaper, 152
Murray, J. Courtney, 164, 165

NATO (North Atlantic Treaty Organization), 95
NCWC (National Catholic Welfare Conference), 63-66, 84, 153
New Yorker, magazine, 152
Newspapers, read by bishops, 151-154
Newsweek, magazine, 152
New Zealand, 81, 157
North Africa, 76
North America, 49, 82, 84, 158; bishops from, 85; periti from, 86, 87
Nyassa, 49

Observers, and bishops, 94; interviewed, 161-62; and Italian bishops, 95; opinions of, 162-74
Oriental bishops, 81
Oriental churches, 114, 119
Osservatore Romano, 47, 48, 152
Ottaviani, A., Cardinal, 123, 124
Our Lady, schema on, 124

Pakistan, 81
Panama, 50, 80
Paraguay, 72, 80, 157
Participation, of bishops in the council, 103-05
Paul VI, Pope, 52, 172
Periti, 87-94, 154, 159, 186; from Italy, 88-90; and mis-

sionary bishops, 90-93; new role of, 91-92; and observers, 163-65
Periodicals, read by bishops, 151-154
Peru, 50
Philippines, 49, 60, 72; bishops from, 49, 50, 75, 80, 81, 116, 131
Piazza S. Ufficio, 73
Pius XI, 30; and the council, 47-48
Pius XII, 26, 30, 37; and the council, 44-47
Pluralism, in the church, 113
Poland, 50; bishops from, 75, 76, 81, 118, 124, 145, 148
Pope, and conciliar sessions, 167-69; and Italian episcopate, 57-58
Portugal, 49; bishops from, 74, 82, 125-26, 148, 160, 163
Presbyterians, 97
Press, impact on bishops, 150-54
Press office, 153, 178
Primacy, of Pope, 168; and collegiality, 171
Protestants, 28, 146; and ecumenism, 95-98; in Spain, 97

Quotidiano, newspaper, 152
Rahner, K., 88, 89, 163
Rassegna della Stampa, 153
Ratzinger, G., 88, 163
Readings, of bishops on the council, 150
Representatives, of bishops interviewed, 18; in the council, 59-61
Rhodesia, 49, 72, 76, 80, 135, 140
Rock, J., Dr., 135